YOUR INNER BILLIONAIRE

Debbie Dobbins

YOUR INNER BILLIONAIRE

Copyright © 2024 by Debbie Dobbins

All rights reserved. No part of this book may be reproduced by any mechanical, photographic, or electronic process, or in the form of a phonographic recording, nor may be stored in a retrieval system, transmitted, or otherwise be copied for public or private use – other than for fair use as brief quotations embodied in articles and reviews – without prior written permission of the publisher.

The author of this book does not dispense medical or spiritual advice or prescribe the use of any technique as a form of treatment for physical, emotional, medical or financial problems without the advice of a physician, accountant, either directly or indirectly. The intent of the author is only to offer information of a general nature to help you in your quest for emotional, physical and spiritual well-being. In the event you use any of the information in this book for yourself, the author and the publisher assume no responsibility for your actions.

For information contact:

Debbie Dobbins
https://thedebbiedobbins.com

Book and Cover design by Designer Jennifer Meller

ISBN: 979-8-9923327-0-4

First Edition: January, 2025

ACKNOWLEDGEMENTS

To my beloved family, whose role in my life has been both challenge and catalyst for growth. Your presence has shaped every aspect of my journey, teaching me lessons that became the foundation of this work. To my mother, whose unwavering love and belief in me remained steadfast through addiction, recovery, and transformation - you've been my constant champion even when I couldn't champion myself.

Special thanks to my spiritual teachers and mentors who guided me through my darkest moments and highest triumphs. Your wisdom helped me translate my experiences into teachings that could serve others. To my first spiritual teacher who told me to "get over myself" - your tough love cracked open my understanding of true prosperity.

To the incredible individuals within the recovery community who shared their journeys with me - your courage and transformation inspired every page of this book. To my clients and students who trusted me with their own prosperity journeys, your breakthroughs and insights enriched this work beyond measure.

And finally, to every angel who passed through my life - the nurses during cancer treatment, the IRS agents who became unlikely allies, the strangers who became guides - your presence in my story helped shape these teachings in ways I never could have imagined.

This book is a testament to the truth that our greatest challenges often become our greatest gifts, and every person who touches our life leaves an imprint on our teaching.

TABLE OF CONTENTS

ACKNOWLEDGEMENTS iii
PROLOGUE vii
INTRODUCTION: AWAKENING YOUR NATURAL PROSPERITY ix
    Why This Matters Now x
    The Abundance Paradox xi
    The Truth About Prosperity xi
    Your Awakening Journey xii
    The Promise xiv
    Your Abundance Birthright xv
    Your Commitment to the Journey xvi
    Your Journey Begins xvii

Chapter 1: THE AWAKENING 1
    The Moment Everything Changed 1
    The Get Over Yourself Moment 4
    Understanding Abundance Consciousness 4
    The Spiritual Principles Behind Prosperity 7
    How the Universe Responds to Our Beliefs 10
    Rewriting Your Money Story 13

Chapter 2: BREAKING FREE FROM SCARCITY 15
    The Prison of Limiting Beliefs 15
    Understanding the Scarcity Mindset 16
    Your Money Story Moments 21
    How Beliefs Shape Our Financial Reality 22
    The Biology of Beliefs 31

Your Money Story Liberation Map 33

Chapter 3: HEALING YOUR MONEY WOUNDS 35
The Liberation Path 35
The Mind Body Connection in Financial Healing 40
Somatic Practices for Financial Transformation 44
Creating New Neuropathways for Wealth 47
The Money Date – Building Conscious Relationship with Wealth 50
Building Trust with Abundance 52
Daily Practices for Lasting Transformation 54

Chapter 4: THE SCIENCE AND FOUNDATION OF GRATITUDE 57
Why Your Brain Loves to Say Thank You 57
The Science Behind Why Gratitude Works 58
The Biology of Blessing 58
The Quantum Connection 59
The Body-Mind Bridge 60
The Quantum Dance of Gratitude 60
Your Body's Abundance Antenna 61
The Evidence Lab 62
The Sacred Science Sweet Spot 63

Chapter 5: BUILDING YOUR ABUNDANCE FOUNDATION 65
The Gratitude Gateway 65
Finding Gratitude in Dark Times 67
The Natural Rhythms of Gratitude 69
Daily Sacred Practices 73

Chapter 6: THE FLOW OF GIVING 76
Understanding Spiritual Economics 76
Learning to Give When I Had Nothing 80

Chapter 7: ACTIVATING YOUR INNER BILLIONAIRE 91
The Universal Laws of Prosperity 92

    How Synchronicity Began Appearing 95
    Meditation and Visualization Practices 97
    Creating a Prosperity Consciousness 100
    The Daily Abundance Alignment Practice 103

Chapter 8: THE LANGUAGE OF WEALTH 105
    How Words Shape Your Financial Reality 105
    Creating Real Affirmations That Actually Work 110
    Creating Your Prosperity Declarations 113

Chapter 9: LIVING IN ABUNDANCE 116
    Setting Prosperity Goals 116
    Dream Bigger Than You Think Possible 117
    From Impossible Dreams to Reality 121
    Creating Clear Intentions 127

Chapter 10: MAINTAINING THE ABUNDANCE MINDSET 140
    Dealing with Setbacks and Fear 140
    How I Handle Challenges Now 143
    Creating Support Systems 145
    Building Lasting Prosperity Habits 148
    Your Daily Abundance Practice 150

Chapter 11: BECOMING THE INNER BILLIONAIRE 154
    My Final Transformation Story 155
    The Ripple Effect of Abundance 157
    Paying it Forward 159
    Living Your Highest Prosperity Potential 160

ABOUT THE AUTHOR 163

PROLOGUE

"Abundance has to come all the way up and from your toe nails."
Debbie Dobbins

Just a few weeks before Thanksgiving, 2017, the world was in unprecedented turmoil. Donald Trump's first year as the 45th president had left the country perilously divided. Social media feeds blazed with political warfare, families stopped speaking to each other over ideological differences, and an atmosphere of uncertainty hung over the nation like a heavy fog. But my personal earthquake happened in a sterile medical office in Pasadena, when my soon-to-retire gastroenterologist stuck his finger up my bum and, coming uncomfortably close to my face, unceremoniously announced, "Yep, it's rectal cancer."

The earth spun on its axis. Everything I thought I knew about wealth, success, and abundance suddenly felt meaningless. I'd built 6 successful businesses, helped countless others achieve their dreams of homeownership, traveled the world doing what I loved, even paid off a seemingly impossible half million dollar IRS debt. I thought I understood transformation. I was wrong.

The drive home was surreal - just a few miles that felt like crossing dimensions. My mind raced with questions: How would I pay for treatment without health insurance? Would I survive? What did true wealth even mean? But something else was happening too - a deeper knowing was emerging, one that would transform my understanding of abundance forever.

Before I even reached home, the doctor called. My blood count was dangerously low. I needed an immediate transfusion. Where does one get that? Walmart? The absurdity of the moment almost made me laugh. Almost.

Here I was, someone who had taught others about abundance, facing the ultimate scarcity - of time, of health, of certainty. Yet in that moment of complete stripping away, I discovered something extraordinary: When everything external is threatened, you finally discover what true wealth means.

This book isn't just about how to get more "STUFF", though we'll certainly explore that. It's about what I learned when cancer forced me to redefine everything - success, wealth, prosperity, and most importantly, gratitude. It's about discovering your inner billionaire not through accumulation, but through appreciation. Not through getting more, but through awakening to what's already here.

The journey that followed would teach me that abundance isn't something we achieve - it's something we uncover. That gratitude isn't just a practice - it's a gateway. That our bodies know more about manifesting prosperity than our minds ever will.

Whether you're facing your own crisis, feeling stuck in scarcity, or simply ready to transform your relationship with abundance, this book offers a path. Not through force or strategy, but through awakening to the prosperity that's already within you.

Your Inner Billionaire is waiting. Let's begin.

Introduction
AWAKENING YOUR NATURAL PROSPERITY

I've made and lost more money than most people will see in a lifetime. I've written millions in mortgages, helped countless others achieve their dreams of homeownership, paid off hundreds of thousands in IRS debt, and created successful businesses from nothing. I've also been so broke I had to buy Christmas dinner from the dollar store, lost everything to addiction, and started over more times than I can count.

But here's the truth I discovered through all the cycles of prosperity and poverty: Creating wealth has nothing to do with your current circumstances and everything to do with accessing your Inner Billionaire-that part of you that inherently understands abundance, naturally attracts opportunities, and knows how to manifest prosperity.

I remember the exact moment this truth cracked open for me. I was sitting in a financial freedom class, drowning in IRS debt that seemed insurmountable, feeling like the biggest fraud in the room. While others shared their money challenges, I thought, "These people don't know what real problems are. I owe the government more than most people make in a lifetime."

Then my teacher looked me straight in the eyes and said three words that would change everything: "Get over yourself." Well she didn't exactly say that, but that is what I heard. She was an incredible spiritual teacher and those were not her words, however that was what I heard. Sometimes we just need a swift kick in the pants to awaken to our truth.

In that moment, something profound shifted. My financial situation wasn't my identity. My debt wasn't who I was. My past wasn't my future. Beneath all the stories of struggle, beneath all the patterns of lack, beneath all the evidence of limitation - there was a part of me that knew how to create abundance. An inner knowing of wisdom that we all have, but have buried it so deeply it takes an awakening to remember it or a shovel.

This inner knowing wasn't unique to me. I've since witnessed it in thousands of others - that spark of prosperity consciousness waiting to be awakened. Whether they were facing bankruptcy or building empires, this Inner Billionaire was present, ready to emerge when given the chance.

Why This Matters Now

We live in a world of unprecedented possibility. Never before have there been so many ways to create wealth, so many opportunities for prosperity, so many paths to abundance. Yet never before have so many people felt so stuck, so limited, so far from their financial potential.

I see this paradox play out every day:

Brilliant entrepreneurs who keep sabotaging success
Talented professionals who can't break through income ceilings
Gifted healers who struggle to charge what they're worth
Creative visionaries who can't translate their gifts into abundance

These aren't people lacking capability - they're people who haven't yet connected with their Inner Billionaire.

The Abundance Paradox

Here's something that used to baffle me: How could I be so good at creating wealth for others through my businesses while simultaneously drowning in my own financial chaos? How could I understand prosperity principles well enough to teach them, yet still find myself buying Christmas dinner at the dollar store?

This is the abundance paradox: We can have all the knowledge, skills, and opportunities for creating wealth, yet still remain stuck in scarcity. We can make millions and lose millions, help others achieve their dreams while sabotaging our own, understand prosperity intellectually while living in limitation.

The traditional approach - focusing on strategies, behaviors, and technical knowledge - misses the crucial point: If you can't access your Inner Billionaire, no strategy will create lasting abundance. It's like having a high-performance car but no key to start it.

The Truth About Prosperity

Think of your Inner Billionaire like a diamond buried beneath layers of limiting beliefs, family patterns, and societal conditioning. The diamond isn't becoming a diamond - it already is one. It just needs to be excavated. Look at nature. Does the ocean worry about running out of waves?

Does the sun fret about conserving rays? Does an apple tree strategize about producing fruit? Nature inherently operates from abundance, constantly creating, constantly giving, constantly flowing. You are not separate from this abundant universe - you are an expression of it, **hell you are one with it!**

This truth hit me profoundly during my darkest moment. I was sitting in my tiny apartment after another financial rock bottom, eating dollar store cookies dipped in frosting (my first addiction). Even in that moment of apparent scarcity, something in me knew I could create whatever my heart desired regardless of money. That knowing wasn't wishful thinking - it was my Inner Billionaire speaking.

Your Inner Billionaire doesn't really care about money. I know that sounds crazy since you probably picked up this book to have more of it. Your Inner Billionaire isn't about having a specific amount of money. It's about having ACCESS to the part of you that:

Sees opportunities where others see obstacles
Creates solutions where others see problems
Attracts resources naturally and easily
Knows how to turn ideas into reality
Understands the flow of abundance

You may have had glimpses of her already:

Times when money flowed effortlessly
Moments when opportunities appeared perfectly
Periods when abundance felt natural
Instances when you created something from nothing

These weren't accidents or flukes. They were glimpses of your true abundant nature breaking through.

Your Awakening Journey

Every transformation has its catalysts - moments when possibility breaks through limitation. For me, there were many: that "get over yourself" moment in financial freedom class, the profound peace I found during my year on food stamps during cancer treatment, the day I finally settled with the IRS. Each built upon the last, gradually revealing what prosperity consciousness truly means.

You see it's not a one and done, get rich quick relationship with your Inner Billionaire. It is a life long journey to live.

This book is designed to create similar breakthrough moments for you. Not just one, but a series of awakenings that compound and expand. You will discover how to:

Break free from scarcity thinking that keeps you trapped
Build an unshakeable abundance foundation
Access your natural prosperity consciousness
Maintain abundance awareness through any challenge

What makes this book different is that it's not about:

- Getting rich quick
- Magical thinking
- Denying current reality
- Following rigid rules

Instead, it's about:

- Awakening your natural prosperity consciousness
- Aligning with universal principles
- Creating sustainable abundance
- Living from your Inner Billionaire's wisdom

Throughout our journey, I'll share stories from my own path as well as others who have met their Inner Billionaire - not just the triumphs but the trials, not just the successes but the setbacks. Because real transformation isn't about achieving perfection; it's about accessing your inner wisdom even through life's challenges.

This brings us to the book's deepest promise...

The Promise

Let me be clear about what this book delivers. Through these pages, you'll experience a complete transformation in your relationship with abundance. Here's exactly what you can expect:

First, you'll discover how to recognize and release the limiting beliefs that have shaped your financial reality. This isn't about blame or shame - it's about freedom. You'll understand why your current situation, whatever it is, isn't a life sentence but a starting point.

Next, you'll learn practical tools that actually work - beginning with the gratitude gateway that opens all doors to prosperity, and moving into the powerful flow of giving. These aren't just nice ideas; they're proven practices that reshape your entire relationship with abundance.

You'll master specific techniques for:

Maintaining prosperity consciousness through any challenge
Recognizing abundance opportunities when they appear
Creating wealth from authentic inspiration
Building sustainable financial freedom
Turning setbacks into setups for greater success

But here's what makes this journey different - you'll discover how to:

Access your natural prosperity consciousness without forcing
Create from abundance rather than scarcity
Give from authenticity rather than obligation
Build wealth while maintaining integrity
Help others awaken their Inner Billionaire

Most importantly, you'll never see yourself the same way again. Once you recognize and connect with your Inner Billionaire, you can't un- know this truth about yourself.

Your Abundance Birthright

You are an expression of an abundant universe. Just as every acorn contains the blueprint for a mighty oak, you contain the blueprint for prosperity. It's literally in your spiritual DNA.

This isn't metaphysical theory - it's scientific fact. The universe is constantly expanding, creating, and expressing abundance. From the multiplying of cells to the spinning of galaxies, increase is the natural order. You're not just living in this abundant universe - you're made of it. Read that sentence again! **You're made of it!!!!**

The evidence of your abundance birthright shows up as:

- Your natural creativity
- Your ability to find solutions
- Your capacity to bounce back
- Your power to generate ideas
- Your drive to grow and expand

Understanding prosperity as your birthright changes everything:

- You don't have to become prosperous - you are prosperous
- You don't have to make yourself worthy - you are worthy
- You don't have to force abundance - you allow it
- You don't have to create wealth - you express it

This understanding becomes the foundation for everything that follows. Instead of trying to add something you lack, you're removing what blocks your natural expression. Instead of forcing yourself to become something different, you're allowing yourself to be who you truly are.

Think of it like a rosebud. The rose doesn't need permission to bloom - it's simply expressing its nature. You are that rose. Your prosperity is as natural as its blooming. Your abundance is as inherent as its fragrance.

Your Commitment to the Journey

This book isn't just to be read - it's an experience to be lived. Each chapter builds upon the last, creating a complete system for awakening your Inner Billionaire. To get the most from this journey I invite you to create an environment for this transformation. It only takes 3 simple steps to create a fertile space for your Inner Billionaire to grow.

1. A Sacred Space
- Prioritize and dedicate time specifically for this experience
- Gift yourself a special prosperity journal, just for this experience.
- Carve out a quiet place for the sacred action
- Honor this as priority time just for you

2. A Commitment to be Consistent
- Taste each chapter as though it were a delicious meal
- Engage with the processes with wholeheartedness
- Create daily rituals
- Document your progress

3. A Promise to Yourself
Take out your journal and complete these statements:

"I am beginning this journey because..."
"I choose to awaken my Inner Billionaire by..."
"I commit to discovering..."
"I am ready to allow..."

Date and sign your promise. Keep this as a touchstone for your journey. Your future self will thank you for this moment of commitment.

Your Journey Begins

Right now, in this moment, you're making a choice. Not just to read a book, but to:

- Awaken to your prosperity nature
- Align with abundance principles
- Access your inner wisdom
- Allow your natural wealth to express

Remember: This journey isn't about becoming something you're not. It's about awakening who you've always been.

Turn the page. Your Inner Billionaire awaits.

Chapter 1
THE AWAKENING

The Moment Everything Changed

I sat in the back of a Financial Freedom class in November 2000, mentally tallying my impossible debt. $350,000 owed to the IRS and another $70,000 in credit cards and business loans. The fluorescent lights buzzed overhead as I shifted uncomfortably in my metal folding chair, trying to make myself smaller, less visible. My mind was doing what minds do best - building a case for why my situation was different, special, worse than anyone else's.

The world outside had just survived Y2K - that much-feared computer apocalypse that never came. The dot-com bubble was bursting, throwing Silicon Valley into chaos. People were still debating the controversial Bush-Gore election, with Florida's hanging chads making headlines. But my personal world felt far removed from these global dramas. While others worried about their tech stocks crashing, I was drowning in debt that had been accumulating since the Reagan administration.

The room smelled like coffee and hope - that peculiar scent of personal development workshops where people come believing transformation is possible. The other participants clutched their Starbucks cups (which had just raised prices to $3 for a latte, causing nationwide grumbling) and eagerly took notes about financial freedom. But I knew better. Or thought I did.

As other participants shared their money challenges - credit card debt, underwater mortgages, struggling businesses - I felt a familiar smugness creep in. A woman near the front was crying about her $20,000 in credit card debt.

Your Inner Billionaire

Another participant worried about a $50,000 business loan. I remember thinking, "These people don't know what real problems are. I could solve their issues in my sleep. But my situation? That's impossible."

I'd been here before - not just in this type of classroom, but in this type of moment. Years earlier, I sat in a different room, convinced my cocaine addiction was uniquely impossible to overcome. Before that, it was the food addiction, sneaking chocolate chips from my mother's cupboard at 8 years old certain I was broken in ways no one could understand.

Then my teacher, a woman who would become one of my greatest mentors, stopped mid-sentence. She walked to the back of the room, planted herself directly in front of my chair, and looked me straight in the eyes. The room went silent as she said three words that would change everything: "Get over yourself." I must confess here she did not say those exact words. She was one of the most loving and supportive humans on the planet, but she was firm and solid in her knowingness that what I and all the rest of the students were going through was an illusion of our own limitations. No one's struggle was any larger in the eyes of the universal consciousness than any of the others. It was what my mind heard - "get over yourself", that flipped the switch for me.

Time seemed to stop. Those three words cut through years of financial victim stories, through layers of "my situation is different" thinking, through the carefully constructed case for why I couldn't succeed. More than that, they cut through a lifetime of making myself special through my struggles.

The irony wasn't lost on me. I'd built a successful mortgage business helping others achieve their dreams. I understood finance intimately. I knew how to create wealth - had done it multiple times and helped countless others do it too. Yet I'd convinced myself that my own situation was beyond help.

Here's what made this moment different from all the other personal development workshops, all the other motivational speeches, all the other "you can do it" moments: I suddenly saw that my very conviction about the impossibility of my situation was what made it impossible. And the good news is that is what makes it possible for YOU!

But it wasn't until years later, lying in a hospital bed being treated for cancer, that I understood the deeper truth about transformation. During a session with a psychic healer, my father (who had passed) came through with a message that would put all my "impossible" situations in a new light.

He showed me what I now refer to as "the Bus Stop conversation". I was able to see a gathering of souls before my birth, planning their earthly missions. In this vision, I saw my father raising his hand, volunteering to play the heart wrenching, bastard role in my life. Not from cruelty, but from love. Every difficulty, every struggle, every seeming obstacle was actually perfectly designed to help me become who I needed to be. When he shared how much love he had to have for me in order to play that role, I was suddenly swept up by this unconditional love and put every experience in my life into perspective. There was only my highest good that was given despite the perceived outward appearances.

"Honey," he said through the healer, "I had to show up that way so you could develop the strength, the resilience, the determination to do what you came here to do. Even this cancer - it's not a punishment. It's an awakening."

As I lay there, tubes running into my arms, weaker than I'd ever been, something profound shifted. What if nothing had gone wrong? What if every seemingly impossible situation - the addiction, the debt, the illness - was actually guided by a deeper wisdom than my human mind could comprehend?

I thought back to that classroom moment, to those three words - "get over yourself." Getting over myself didn't mean dismissing my challenges. It meant getting over the story that my challenges made me special, different, beyond help. It meant recognizing that feeling unique in our struggles is the very thing that keeps us struggling.

That day in the financial freedom class wasn't just about money. It was about recognizing a fundamental truth: We are the creators of our reality. Not sometimes. Not just in certain areas. ALWAYS! Our situations aren't special. Our problems aren't unique. But our power to transform them is unlimited - once we get over ourselves enough to access it.

The Get Over Yourself Moment

Now it's your turn to reveal your "Get Over Yourself Moment". Take your journal, settle into your sacred space and journal on these questions:

Your "Impossible" Inventory:
1. List three situations you currently believe are "impossible"
2. For each one, write: "This is impossible because..."
3. Now write: "What if it's impossible because I believe it is?"

Your Past Transformations:
1. List three "impossible" situations you've already overcome
2. What made them seem impossible at the time?
3. What shifted to make transformation possible?
4. What beliefs changed in the process?

Your Current Invitation:
1. What situation is asking you to "get over yourself" right now?
2. What story about being "special" or "different" are you ready to release?
3. What new possibility opens up when you let go of this story?

Understanding Abundance Consciousness

That classroom awakening was just the beginning. What followed was a profound shift in how I understood abundance itself. It's easy to think prosperity consciousness is about positive thinking or manifesting magic. It's not. It's about recognizing a fundamental truth about who you truly are.

Think about nature for a moment. Does the ocean worry about running out of waves? Does the sun fret about conserving its rays? Does an apple tree strategize about producing fruit? Nature inherently operates from abundance, constantly creating, constantly giving, constantly flowing. And guess what? **You are Nature!!!!**

I discovered this truth in the most unlikely place - during my recovery from addiction. I noticed that the more I shared my story with others, the more my own healing deepened. The more I gave support, the more supported I felt. The more I allowed love to flow out, the more it flowed in. This is a universal law that what you give you receive. **It's immutable.**

This same principle applied to money, though it took me years to see it. When I held onto every dollar in fear, believing there would never be enough, I created constriction. During my darkest financial times, I discovered something profound: even when I had almost nothing materially, I could still participate in the flow of giving. Sometimes it was just a genuine smile, a moment of presence, a word of encouragement.

Let me share a pivotal moment that illustrates this. During my cancer treatment, when I was living on food stamps, I had exactly enough money for either a cup of coffee or bus fare home. Standing in line at the coffee shop, I caught myself in some desperate scarcity thinking: "I can't afford this... I shouldn't be here... What if I need this money later?"

Then I remembered: consciousness creates reality. In that moment, I chose to buy the coffee and enjoy it fully - not from recklessness, but from a decision to practice abundance consciousness even with my last few dollars. I savored every sip, blessed the barista, appreciated the experience completely.

Walking home (yes, I walked), something shifted. Instead of feeling deprived, I felt abundant. Instead of focusing on what I lacked, I noticed the wealth of experiences around me - the sunshine, the architecture, the opportunity to exercise. By the time I got home, three unexpected phone calls had come in with money from places I never imagined, a refund check which had never been cashed, an overpayment on an outstanding bill and a gift from a previous client.

This wasn't coincidence. It was the law of consciousness at work. Just as my conviction about my "impossible" IRS situation had created that reality, my shift to abundance consciousness - even in a seemingly small moment - created new possibilities.

The most beautiful evidence of this came during my IRS negotiation years earlier. Instead of approaching it from fear and shame (my previous consciousness), I chose to see everyone involved as partners in resolution. This included the IRS agent who became an unexpected ally, the tax attorney who found creative solutions, even the debt itself, which I began to thank for its lessons.

From this new consciousness, what seemed impossible began resolving naturally. The final settlement was pennies on the dollar - not because I manipulated anything, but because my consciousness had shifted from resistance to flow.

It's time for you to take a deep breath and look at what your current consciousness is towards your good, wealth and abundance:

Take Out Your Journal, get comfy in your sacred space and journal your awareness of:

Consciousness Tracking

1. Daily Consciousness Check:
Track your money interactions for one day

- Note your immediate thoughts/feelings about:
- Paying bills

- Making purchases
- Receiving money
- Finding money
- Spending decisions

2. Shift Practice:

Instead of: "I can't afford this"
Practice: "I'm choosing to invest in..."

Instead of: "There's never enough"
Practice: "Money flows to me in expected and unexpected ways"

Instead of: "I have to..."
Practice: "I choose to..."

3. Evidence Collection:
- Note three times abundance showed up unexpectedly
- Record how you felt in those moments
- What consciousness preceded these experiences?

The Spiritual Principles Behind Prosperity

The universe speaks to us in many ways, but none more clear than when we're being guided to our next level of growth. Let me share two profound examples that taught me this truth.

I had been born and raised in So. California and was very rooted there. I took a trip to see my brother in Texas. Each night as I layed in my 8-year old nephew's bunk bed, I began hearing an inner voice with crystal clarity: "Move to Texas." Not a vague notion, but a persistent, specific directive. The voice was so strong it would keep me awake at night, repeating like a mantra: "Move to Texas, Move to Texas." Not matter how many times I asked it to literally "shut up", it persisted.

My analytical mind immediately jumped to all the reasons this was impossible. I had no job in Texas, no place to live, no car and most importantly - my grandmother's 500-pound piano was in my condo in California and impossible to move. This piano became my go-to excuse, my shield against change. Every time the voice said "Move to Texas," I'd respond, "But what about the piano?" Sound silly? Well we all have our silly excuses and they only need to make sense to us. Take a minute and remember some of your own.

Looking back now, it's almost comical how I used this piano as my reason to resist divine guidance. Here I was, being called to a complete life transformation, and I was letting half a ton of wood and strings stop me. But isn't that what we often do? Find the one "impossible" obstacle and make it our reason for staying stuck?

The moment I finally surrendered - truly surrendered - everything fell into place with remarkable synchronicity. Not only did I find a way to move the piano, I was packed in a Ryder truck within one week after returning back to California. I told myself not to look in the rear-view mirror on the 3-day trip to Texas, as I was sure I would turn around. Landing on my brother's couch, buying a $500 jalopy, I had a job in a very challenging job market within a week. The next few years I created the first female owned and operated mortgage company in that small town in Texas and was able to sell the business because of what happened as a result of the IRS experience. The piano that had been my excuse became a symbol of how the universe removes obstacles when we get out of our own way. Even a half a ton of wood and strings were no match for surrendering to spirit.

Perhaps the most powerful demonstration of spiritual principles came during my cancer journey. Imagine this scene: I'm sitting in my doctor's office, having just been diagnosed with rectal cancer, and he's telling me I have critically low blood counts requiring immediate transfusions. No health insurance. No savings. Just the stark reality of a life-threatening condition and seemingly no way to get care.

When I called my mother in panic mode about needing blood transfusions, her response was surprisingly simple: "Just go to the emergency room, honey. They can't turn you away." In that moment of complete vulnerability, this straightforward guidance cut through all my fear and complexity. You see we need moms and mentors in our lives to remind us of our possibilities.

What unfolded next was nothing short of miraculous. Not only was I admitted to one of the best hospitals in Pasadena, but I was given a beautiful room with a view of the San Gabriel mountains. The care team that assembled around me was exceptional. A woman appeared in my room and asked if I was "poor enough" to qualify for California's Medicaid program. Heck yes I was, and every single aspect of my treatment - from emergency surgery to radiation to the longest hospital stay imaginable - was completely covered.

But here's what really brings me to tears when I think about it: The quality of care I received wasn't just adequate - it was extraordinary. The universe didn't just provide the basics; it provided the best possible care at exactly the right time. Every need was met, every door opened, every resource appeared.

These experiences taught me something profound about spiritual principles: They don't just work sometimes, or only for some people, or only in certain situations. **They work always, for everyone, in every situation** - when we align with them. The key is getting ourselves out of the way.

In both these experiences - the piano and the cancer journey - I witnessed what I now call the Three Principles of Divine Support:

First, Perfect Divine Timing. My resistance to moving to Texas was an obstacle until I finally surrendered. When I did, everything happened with lightning speed. Similarly, my cancer diagnosis came at exactly the right moment when California's healthcare system could support me fully. Had it been a year earlier or later, the circumstances might have been completely different.

Second, Perfect Provision. Not only did I receive what I needed, but I received it in ways far beyond what I could have orchestrated myself. A beautiful hospital room with a mountain view might seem like a small detail, but it was spirit's way of saying, "I'm not just handling your survival; I'm caring for your soul."

Third, Perfect Guidance. That persistent voice about Texas, my mother's simple advice about the emergency room - these weren't just random thoughts or communications. They were divine guidance cutting through the complexity my human mind wanted to create. If we are open to receiving answers they will be provided.

How the Universe Responds to Our Beliefs

This brings us to perhaps the most crucial understanding about prosperity consciousness: The universe doesn't respond to what we want or what we think we deserve. It responds to what we believe is possible.

When I believed my IRS debt was insurmountable, every attempt to resolve it failed. When I believed I couldn't possibly move without first solving the piano problem, I stayed stuck. But the moment my beliefs shifted - often through what seemed like crisis or desperation - the universe revealed solutions that had been there all along.

The most profound demonstration of how the universe responds to our beliefs came during my IRS situation. For years, the $350,000 tax debt felt like a life sentence. Why? Because I believed it was. Every time I looked at the numbers, my mind would spin out into impossibility thinking: "No one could ever resolve this much debt." "The IRS never negotiates." "I'll be paying this until I die."

Then came that moment in the financial freedom class - "Get over yourself." Something cracked open. If I could overcome cocaine addiction, if I could rebuild my life from nothing multiple times, why was I so convinced this particular challenge was insurmountable?

I began approaching the IRS differently. Instead of hiding from them (which I'd done for years), I started seeing them as potential partners in resolution. Instead of assuming they were out to get me, I chose to believe they might be willing to work with me. Most importantly, instead of letting my shame and fear drive my actions, I let my new belief in possibility guide me.

The result? A settlement for pennies on the dollar. The exact same IRS that I'd been running from for years suddenly became reasonable, helpful, even supportive. Nothing had changed about the debt itself - what changed was my belief about what was possible.

This lesson served me profoundly years later when facing cancer without insurance. Because I'd already experienced how the universe responds to our beliefs rather than our circumstances, I was able to trust more quickly, surrender more fully, allow solutions to appear more easily. For years, whenever I received money in birthday cards, I had a predictable pattern. Before even finishing reading the card, my mind would race to which crisis needed solving - which bill was most overdue, which emergency needed addressing. The money would vanish as quickly as it appeared, always into some "emergency."

One birthday, I decided to try something different. I received a $100 bill from a family member and instead of immediately allocating it to problems, I sat with it. I placed the bill in a special spot and each time I looked at it, I practiced feeling abundant rather than needy. Instead of seeing it as a temporary solution to permanent worry, I saw it as evidence of how supported I was.

That $100 stayed with me for months - not because I didn't use it, but because my consciousness about it had shifted from scarcity (it will disappear) to abundance (I am well-supported). More importantly, other money started flowing from unexpected sources. The bill itself became a tool for consciousness practice rather than a temporary band-aid for chronic fear.

Our financial reality isn't created by our bank accounts - it's created by our beliefs about what's possible. Here's how this plays out in real life.

Seemingly small moments - choosing gratitude over fear with a $100 bill, savoring a cup of coffee instead of feeding scarcity thoughts - built the foundation for bigger transformations. Each time I consciously shifted my beliefs about money, the universe responded in increasingly dramatic ways.

Remember that IRS debt I was so convinced was a life sentence? The same consciousness practice that worked with birthday cards and coffee ultimately transformed that situation. Instead of seeing the IRS as an enemy and the debt as impossible, I began treating every interaction with them as an opportunity to practice new beliefs. By incorporating mantras such as, "This situation is solvable", "Solutions appear in unexpected ways", "Everyone involved wants resolution", "I am divinely guided through this process", the how began to reveal itself organically without struggle.

These may seem to be miracles, but in actuality they were the natural result of aligned consciousness.

This is why I'm sharing these stories with you. Your situation might look different from mine. Maybe it's not IRS debt or addiction recovery or health challenges. But the principle remains the same: Your beliefs are creating your financial reality right now. RIGHT NOW! If you want to know what your beliefs are, look around you.

Think about it. What's your equivalent of my "impossible" IRS debt? What situation are you convinced is beyond solution? What if - just like my coffee shop moment proved - abundance is trying to reach you in ways your current beliefs won't let you see?

This is where our real work begins. Before we dive into dismantling your prison of limiting beliefs in the next chapter, you need to clearly see the story you've been telling about money. More importantly, you need to glimpse the new story that's waiting to emerge.

That's why I invite you now to complete the "Your New Money Story" activity below. This isn't just another journaling activity. It's your declaration of readiness to transform your relationship with abundance. Just as my "get over yourself" moment cracked open new possibilities, this exercise can crack open yours.

Remember: The universe isn't responding to what you want or what you think you deserve. It's responding to what you believe is possible. Let's discover what becomes possible when you believe differently.

Are you ready to look at your own Money Story and patterns? Take out your journal, get cozy in your sacred space and write about these questions and ideas.

Rewriting Your Money Story

1. Your Current Story:
- What do you believe about money?
- What patterns keep repeating?
- What limits have you accepted?
- What role do you cast yourself in?

2. Story Revision:
- What new role are you ready to play?
- What becomes possible with new beliefs?
- What patterns are you ready to change?
- What abundance are you ready to allow?

3. Bridge to Freedom:
- What old beliefs are ready to be released?
- What new beliefs are emerging?
- What support would help this transition?
- What first step can you take today?

As you complete the Your New Money Story journaling, you might notice something fascinating: the very act of examining your beliefs begins to loosen their grip. That's because beliefs only maintain their power when they operate unconsciously. By bringing them into the light, you've already begun the process of transformation.

But here's what I've discovered through my own journey from IRS debt to financial freedom, from addiction to awakening, from scarcity to abundance: Seeing our limiting beliefs is just the first step. Next, we must understand how these beliefs became our prison - and more importantly, how to break free from them. That's exactly what we'll explore in the next Chapter: The Prison of Limiting Beliefs.

As we move into this chapter about breaking free from scarcity thinking, remember, awakening is just the beginning. Now that you've glimpsed your Inner Billionaire, now that you've seen evidence of universal support, now that you understand the power of consciousness - it's time to release what no longer serves you.

The prison of limiting beliefs isn't your natural home. It never was. It's simply a structure you've outgrown, like a butterfly ready to leave its chrysalis.

This awakening chapter isn't about reaching a destination - it's about starting a journey. Are you ready to explore how to break free from your limiting beliefs and scarcity patterns that have held you back?

First let's celebrate your awakening. Celebrate the fact that you're reading these words, that something in you recognizes these truths, that your Inner Billionaire is stirring to life.

Your abundance journey has begun. And like all great adventures, it starts with a single step - the step you've just taken by awakening to your true prosperous nature.

Chapter 2

BREAKING FREE FROM SCARCITY

The Prison of Limiting Beliefs

I stared at the number on the IRS notice: $350,000. My hands trembled as I set the paper down on my desk, a cheap particle board piece I'd received as a hand me down from a friend. It was early 2000 and $350,000 was closer to half a million in today's inflation, and it was like a bullet train accumulating penalties and interest. The irony wasn't lost on me – here I was, a mortgage banker who had helped thousands achieve their dreams of homeownership, yet I couldn't achieve the American Dream myself. The IRS debt loomed over me like a dark cloud, making every other financial obligation seem trivial in comparison. After years of telling every client who walked through my door "anyone can get a home loan", I was the one exception as federal liens prevented that and my lien was more than the value of the home.

"I could cure myself of cancer," I remember thinking, "but I'll never get out from under this." Even the smallest dent would be gobbled up by penalties and interest as soon as it was made.

That thought stopped me cold. Where had this thought come from? Why did I believe I could overcome a life-threatening illness but not a financial one? The answer would take years to fully understand, but in that moment, I glimpsed a profound truth: my relationship with money wasn't about the money at all. It was about what I believed was possible.

We all carry these beliefs about money, success, and our worth. They're like invisible prison bars, keeping us confined in patterns of scarcity and lack. Some of us learned them at kitchen tables watching our parents argue about bills. Others absorbed them from society's messages about what we deserve or who gets to be wealthy. These beliefs become the foundation of our financial reality, quietly dictating every decision we make about money – or more accurately, every decision we don't make.

I was living this reality daily in my mortgage business. I could create money seemingly out of thin air, helping clients manifest their homeownership dreams through creative financing solutions. Yet my own massive tax debt loomed over me like a dark cloud, making every other financial obligation seem trivial in comparison. The gap between my ability to generate wealth and my ability to keep it revealed a deeper pattern – one that many of us share but rarely recognize.

Understanding the Scarcity Mindset

This is what a scarcity mindset does: it convinces us that there will never be enough, that we don't deserve abundance, that financial freedom is for "other people." Even when evidence of abundance surrounds us, we stay locked in our prison of limiting beliefs, like a bird that's forgotten it has wings.

Before we can break free from this prison, we need to understand how we built it. Every belief that keeps you stuck in scarcity has a story behind it. My story started long before that IRS looming debt landed in my mailbox. It began with early messages about money, was reinforced through family patterns, and solidified through experiences that seemed to "prove" what I already believed about myself and wealth.

Take a moment now to consider: What's the most persistent thought you have about money? Don't judge it, don't try to make it "positive"– just capture it honestly. This thought, whether you're conscious of it or not, is actively shaping your financial reality right now.

In my world of mortgage banking, I saw this principle play out countless times. Two clients could have identical credit scores, income, and financial circumstances, yet one would manifest their dream home while the other remained stuck in limiting patterns. The difference wasn't in their numbers – it was in their beliefs about what was possible for them.

Throughout this chapter, we'll explore how these beliefs take root, why they're so powerful, and most importantly, how to begin dismantling them. My own journey from crushing debt to financial freedom wasn't just about paying off the IRS or recovering from cancer with no way to pay for it – it's about the fundamental shift in consciousness that made that external change possible.

The prison of scarcity is built one belief at a time. And that's exactly how we'll break free from it – one belief, one story, one shift in consciousness at a time. Your liberation begins with understanding how you got here. Let's start by examining the blueprint of your own financial prison.

The strangest thing about scarcity thinking is how it persists even in the face of abundance. There I was, regularly closing six-figure mortgage deals, creating wealth for others, yet living in a constant state of "not enough." When money came in, I spent it like water through a sieve – expensive client dinners, impulsive purchases, anything to temporarily fill that void of unworthiness. Then I'd turn around and drive a beat-up $500 car, telling myself I didn't deserve better.

This push-pull relationship with money defined my life: periods of abundant income followed by spectacular binges of spending, then retreating into a cave of avoidance and self-denial. I could make money appear almost magically, yet I couldn't seem to keep any of it. The more I made, the faster it disappeared.

Do you have a familiar feeling? Remember it's not the story that matters, it's the feelings you have about your story. This is what scarcity does to your brain.

It creates these paradoxical relationships with money where no matter what you do - spend it or save it, make it or lose it - you never feel secure, never feel like you have enough, never feel worthy of true abundance. It's like wearing dark sunglasses indoors - everything looks dim even when the room is brilliantly lit.

I remember sitting in my office one afternoon, staring at a commission check - it was more money than my parents made in a year. Instead of feeling successful, I immediately started planning ways to spend it, as if having it in my account was somehow dangerous. The same day, I helped a first-time homebuyer with an income 10 times lower than mine qualify for their dream home. I could see true abundance was possible for them, but somehow, I remained convinced it wasn't possible for me.

Your scarcity mindset is not logical, it's psychological. And it shows up in three predictable patterns:

First, there's never enough. No matter how much money you make, it feels like you're always one step away from financial disaster. I called this my "magic disappearing money act" - the more I made, the more quickly it seemed to vanish.

Second, you can see possibility for others but not yourself. As a mortgage banker, I was a master at seeing financial opportunities for my clients. I could creatively structure loans, spot hidden assets, and build compelling cases for their success. Yet when it came to my own finances, I was blind to opportunities staring me in the face.

Third, you're constantly waiting for the other shoe to drop. Even when things are going well, you can't fully enjoy it because you're certain it won't last. I spent years bracing for financial disaster, and guess what? That tension actually created the very problems I feared.

Here's what I didn't understand then but see so clearly now: scarcity isn't about how much money you have. It's about your relationship with what you have.

Some of my wealthiest clients lived in constant fear of loss, while some of my most modest-income clients radiated genuine abundance. It is NEVER about the money, EVER! IT'S ALWAYS ABOUT YOUR RELATIONSHIP WITH YOUR INNER BILLIONAIRE!

The most insidious part? Scarcity becomes a self-fulfilling prophecy. When I believed I couldn't keep money, I made decisions that guaranteed I wouldn't. When I was convinced the IRS debt would destroy me, I stopped taking actions that could have resolved it sooner. When I felt unworthy of success, I unconsciously sabotaged it.

Let's pause here for a moment. Think about your own life. Where is scarcity showing up? Maybe it's in how you order at restaurants, how you shop for groceries, or how you react to unexpected expenses. Maybe it's in the way you deflect compliments about money, downplay your successes, or constantly worry about the future.

The truth is, scarcity is like a lens through which we view every financial decision, every opportunity, every possibility in our lives. Until we recognize this lens, we can't change it. And until we change it, we'll keep creating the same results, no matter how much money we make or how successful we appear to others.

I had to hit my own rock bottom with being shut out from owning my own home, something I did day in and day out, before I could finally see my scarcity lens for what it was – a prison of my own making. But here's the good news: once you recognize these patterns, you've already begun the process of breaking free from them.

The first step isn't even about changing your thoughts – it's about becoming aware of them. Start noticing when scarcity thinking kicks in. Pay attention to the situations that trigger it, the physical sensations that accompany it, the decisions you make from this mindset. This awareness itself begins to loosen scarcity's grip on your life.

You don't have to believe everything you think about money. Those thoughts aren't facts – they're just stories you've been telling yourself for so long that they feel like truth. I promise you, a new story is possible. I've lived it. And in the next section, we'll explore exactly how these beliefs shape our financial reality – and more importantly, how to begin reshaping them.

The devastation of facing up to my IRS lien, wasn't the first time I'd created financial chaos in my life. Looking back, I can see a clear pattern: make money, spend money, avoid money, repeat. But it wasn't until I faced that overwhelming debt that I finally had to ask myself: What beliefs were driving this cycle?

Here's what I discovered: Every financial decision I made was being filtered through beliefs I didn't even know I had. Like invisible software running in the background of my mind, these beliefs were quietly directing my every money move.

Those periods when I'd make fantastic money in my mortgage business, I'd immediately spend it all because deep down, I believed I didn't deserve to keep it. That beat-up car I drove? It wasn't really about being practical - it was about believing I didn't deserve nice things. The way I'd avoid looking at my bank statements? That came from a core belief that I couldn't trust myself with money.

Through my work helping others transform their relationship with money, I've identified four common "fables" or stories if you will, that keep us trapped in scarcity thinking:

1. *The Sacrifice Story: "You have to work hard and suffer to make money"*
2. *The Worthiness Tale: "People like me don't get to be wealthy"*
3. *The Morality Myth: "Money is the root of all evil"*
4. *The Scarcity Saga: "There's never enough to go around"*

Let's pause here for a moment and do something important. Rather than just reading about my patterns, let's uncover yours. Don't worry - this isn't a formal exercise with worksheets and number scales. This is about getting real with yourself.

Your Money Story Moments

Make yourself comfortable in your sacred space and relax your body. Take a few moments to center and then ask yourself these questions:

What were the last three times you made a significant financial decision - good or bad. Maybe it was a purchase, an investment, or even avoiding a financial choice altogether. Either journal them or keep them in your mind. For each one, ask yourself:

- What was the story I was telling myself in that moment?
- What felt "safe" or "dangerous" about this choice?
- What old family messages came up?
- What did this decision say about what I believe I deserve?

Just sit with these questions for a moment. Let your answers surface naturally. It's so important not to overthink these questions. Rather spend time letting your intuition share information with you.

Take a few moments to record them in your journal for reflection later.

For me, this kind of reflection revealed something stunning: I had been operating on beliefs I inherited from my family without ever questioning them. My mother's Depression-era fear of not having enough. My father's pattern of creating financial drama. Both of these shaped my reality because I believed they were truth rather than merely stories I'd absorbed.

But here's where it gets interesting: Your beliefs about money don't just influence your conscious choices - they actually shape what opportunities you can see. When I believed I could never resolve my IRS debt, I became blind to possible solutions. When I believed I didn't deserve lasting success, I unconsciously created situations that proved me right.

Think of it like this: Your beliefs are like a pair of colored glasses. If you're wearing red glasses, everything looks red. If you're wearing scarcity glasses, everything looks like "not enough" - even abundance when it's staring you in the face.

I watched this play out countless times in my mortgage business. Two clients with identical financial situations would walk in my door. One believed homeownership was possible for them; the other was convinced they'd never qualify. Guess whose loan usually went through? It wasn't about the numbers - it was about what they believed was possible. The same was true when I would coach a client on abundance principles.

How Beliefs Shape Our Financial Reality

After decades of research, practical experience and coaching hundreds of humans, I've come to realize that your beliefs create your reality in three specific ways:

First, they filter what you can see. If you believe "money is hard to come by," your brain will literally filter out evidence of easy money opportunities.

Second, they direct your actions. If you believe "I'm bad with money," you'll unconsciously make choices that prove this belief true.

Third, they shape your energy around money. If you believe "I don't deserve wealth," you'll subtly push away financial abundance when it shows up.

I saw all three of these at work in my own life and the lives of so many. Even as I was helping others create wealth through real estate, I was pushing it away in my own life because I didn't believe I deserved it. Even as I was structuring creative financial solutions for clients, I couldn't see those same possibilities for myself because my beliefs told me they weren't available to me.

The good news? Beliefs aren't facts. They're just thoughts we've thought so many times that they feel like truth. And thoughts can change.

But here's what's crucial to understand: You can't change beliefs you don't know you have. That's why awareness is the first step toward transformation. Before we can create new financial realities, we need to understand what beliefs are currently creating our money story.

Let's take this exploration deeper with what I call "The Belief Detective" process. This is an adventure in self-discovery. For the next few days, simply notice:

1. What do you consistently say about money?
2. What financial situations make you uncomfortable?
3. What money patterns keep repeating in your life?
4. What feels "impossible" for you financially?

Don't try to change anything yet. Just notice. Write it down if you want, or just keep a mental note. The key is becoming aware of the invisible beliefs that have been running your financial show.

Your current financial reality isn't a reflection of your worth or potential. It's simply a reflection of your beliefs about what's possible for you. And beliefs can change. I know because I've lived it and watched it with hundreds of my coaching clients. The IRS lien, being broke after cancer, all that seemed impossible to resolve? Once I changed my beliefs about what was possible, solutions began appearing that I couldn't see before.

But before we talk about changing beliefs, we need to understand the most common limiting beliefs that keep us stuck. When I finally started examining my beliefs about money, I discovered something fascinating: the stories I told myself weren't actually original. They were like greatest hits from a universal playlist of limiting beliefs that most of us download early in life.

Take my personal favorite: "I can make money, but I can't keep it." This belief played on repeat in my head for decades. I was the queen of manifesting money out of thin air, then watching it vanish just as quickly. I could close major deals on Monday and avoid opening the bills in the mailbox by Friday.

Here's another classic that ruled my life: "If I become too successful, people won't like me." This one was particularly sneaky because it disguised itself as humility. I'd downplay my achievements, take less than I deserved, even sabotage opportunities - all while telling myself I was being "humble."

Let's look at the top five limiting beliefs I've seen destroy more financial dreams than any market crash ever could:

1. "Money and spirituality don't mix."
This was my go-to excuse for financial chaos. I convinced myself that my money problems somehow made me more spiritually evolved. Meanwhile, I was causing harm to myself and others through my irresponsible financial behavior. Real spirituality includes having a healthy relationship with money.

2. "I have to struggle to succeed."
How many times did I choose the hard way because I believed anything that came easily wasn't valid? I literally created struggles to prove I was worthy of success. The IRS debt? Part of me believed I needed that mountain to climb to prove my worth.

3. "Someone else will save me/solve this."
Even while running my own successful business, I secretly hoped someone would swoop in and fix my financial messes. This belief kept me from taking full responsibility for my money story.

4. "I don't understand money."
This was perhaps my most ironic belief. There I was, structuring complex mortgage deals and explaining financial concepts to clients, while telling myself I wasn't good with money. Your intelligence isn't the issue - your beliefs are.

5. "Once I have X amount, then I'll feel secure."
The number kept changing, but the feeling of security never came. Why? Because security isn't about the number in your bank account - it's about your relationship with uncertainty.

Here's where it gets interesting: These beliefs aren't just thoughts - they're prophecies we fulfill without realizing it. When I believed I couldn't keep money, I made choices that guaranteed I wouldn't. When I believed success would make people dislike me, I held myself back in ways that kept me "safe" but stuck.

Let's take a moment here to uncover your own greatest hits. Take a moment and notice how you react or which of these stories feel familiar in your bones:

"Money is the root of all evil"
"Rich people are greedy"
"I have to work hard for every penny"
"I'll never be good with money"
"Money goes to money"
"I don't deserve to be wealthy"

As you read each one, notice your body's response. Does your chest tighten? Does your breath get shallow? Does your stomach clench? Your body knows your truth before your mind admits it.

Here's the tricky part about limiting beliefs: they often disguise themselves as wisdom. "I'm being responsible" might really be "I'm afraid to take risks." "I'm not materialistic" might really be "I don't believe I deserve abundance."

I remember the day this hit home for me. I was sitting with a client who was afraid to buy a home because "it's irresponsible to take on debt." Meanwhile, she was paying more in rent than a mortgage would cost. Her "responsible" belief was actually keeping her from building wealth because of her fear and lack of self-worth.

That's when I realized: Every limiting belief about money is really a prison guard, keeping us locked in patterns of scarcity. These beliefs feel like they're protecting us, but they're actually preventing us from experiencing true financial freedom.

But here's what's amazing: Once you identify these beliefs, they begin to lose their power. It's like turning on the light and realizing the monster in your room is just a pile of clothes. The fear isn't gone immediately, but now you know it's not real.

This awareness creates a crack in the prison wall. And through that crack, new possibilities start to appear. That's exactly what happened with my IRS burden. Once I identified and questioned my limiting beliefs about it, solutions I couldn't see before started becoming visible.

Remember: These beliefs aren't facts - they're stories. And stories can be rewritten. In fact, that's exactly what we're going to explore next: how to begin rewriting your money story from limitation to possibility.

But first, I want you to do something powerful: Choose one limiting belief from this section that really resonates with you. The one that made you think "ouch - that's me." Hold onto it, because we're about to discover how to transform it from a prison guard into a doorway to freedom.

But first, let me tell you what happened when I finally faced my own biggest money story - the one about that IRS debt being impossible to resolve.

When I made that statement, "I could cure myself of cancer, but this IRS lien was impossible", I was expecting sympathy, a buy in to my situation, maybe some commiseration about how unfair the system was. Instead, my spiritual teacher looked me straight in the eyes and more or less said "Get over yourself". As I mentioned she did not say those exact words, but my desire for someone to buy into my story was interrupted by her firm but loving feedback that my story was not any different than anyone else's in the room.

I was stunned. And angry. And defensive. And... somewhere deep inside, awakened and knew she was speaking truth.

"You believe you can cure cancer but can't handle this debt? That's not truth - that's drama," she said. "What's the story you're so committed to that you'd rather keep suffering than let it go?"

Boom. There it was. My money story exposed in all its glory.

See, we all have a money story we're committed to. It's like a movie we've watched so many times we can recite every line. My story went something like this: "I'm great at making money, I'll always be in some kind of financial mess. I'm ashamed of every action that has created this mess that I'm in. That's just who I am."

Sound familiar? Maybe your story has different lines, but I bet it feels just as true to you as mine did to me.

Here's the thing about stories though - they're just that. Stories. They're not facts, they're not destiny, and they're definitely not carved in stone. They're simply narratives we've chosen to believe, usually without even realizing we made that choice.

Let's pause here and do something powerful. We're going to identify your current money story. This isn't a formal exercise - think of it more like becoming the narrator of your own life instead of just being a character in it.

Take a moment and complete this sentence: "My story about money is..."

Don't overthink it. Don't try to make it sound good. Just let the truth come out. Maybe your story is "Money always slips through my fingers" or "I'll never be as successful as my siblings" or "Rich people are just lucky", "I've been broke my whole life".

Now contemplate these questions:
1. Where did you first learn this story?
2. How has believing this story affected your choices?
3. What evidence do you have that this story is actually true?
4. What evidence do you have that it might be false?

Now, imagine your relationship with money as a character in a play. Write a brief scene showing how this character typically acts when dealing with financial decisions. What role are they playing? Victim? Martyr? Rebel? Struggler?

When I did this exercise myself, I realized I had been playing the role of the Perpetual Struggler – someone who could never quite get ahead no matter how hard they worked. This role was so ingrained that even when opportunities for abundance presented themselves, I subconsciously sabotaged them to stay in character. When I really dug into my story about being bad at keeping money, I realized I'd inherited it from my father. He was a master at making money disappear - and not in a fun, magician kind of way. I watched him cycle through success and failure so many times that it became my template for "normal."

Got your story? Good. Now here's where it gets interesting.

Ask yourself:
1. Who gave me this story?
2. When did I first start believing it?
3. What evidence do I look for to prove it's true?
4. What evidence do I ignore that might disprove it?

But here's what's fascinating: Once I could see it as a story rather than a truth, I started noticing all the times it wasn't true. Times I had managed money well. Times I'd made smart financial decisions. Times I'd created lasting wealth for others through my mortgage business and teaching the abundance principles I knew to be true.

These examples had always been there, but my story filtered them out. It's like my brain had a "delete" button for any evidence that contradicted my chosen narrative.

This is where real transformation begins - not in trying to force new beliefs, but in questioning our current ones. It's about becoming curious instead of convinced.

When I finally got curious about my humungous tax lien story instead of certain about it, solutions started appearing. People with expertise showed up. Opportunities emerged. Nothing in my external reality had changed yet - but my relationship with what was possible had shifted dramatically.

This is crucial to understand: Your money story isn't just about money. It's about what you believe is possible for you. It's about who you think you are and what you think you deserve.

Let's take this deeper. Look at your money story again, but this time, ask yourself:

1. What does this story protect me from?
2. What does it let me avoid?
3. What would be possible if this story weren't true?
4. Who would I be without this limitation?

When I asked myself these questions about my story, I realized my "impossible to solve" story was protecting me from taking full responsibility for my finances. As long as the situation was "impossible," I didn't have to face my own role in creating it - or my power to change it.

This is where transformation really begins - in these moments of radical honesty with ourselves. Not beating ourselves up, not trying to force positive thinking, but simply seeing our stories for what they are: choices we've made about what to believe NOT WHAT WE HAVE DONE!

And if we can choose what to believe, we can choose to believe differently.

That's exactly what we're going to explore next - how to consciously choose a new story. But remember: You can't rewrite a story you haven't read. So for now, just let yourself become aware of the story you've been telling. Awareness itself is transformative.

Your current money story got you this far. It served a purpose. It protected you in some way. Thank it for its service. And then get ready to write a new chapter - because that's exactly what we're about to do.

You know that moment when you're watching a movie and suddenly realize you've seen this plot before? That's what happened to me the day I recognized my money story wasn't just mine. The characters and settings were different, but the core narrative - this dance between possibility and limitation, between abundance and scarcity - was playing out everywhere I looked.

These stories don't just affect our bank accounts – they impact every aspect of our lives. When I believed I could never overcome tax debt, I:

- *Stopped taking risks that could lead to growth*
- *Avoided looking at my finances altogether*
- *Made decisions from a place of fear rather than possibility*
- *Rejected opportunities that seemed "too good to be true"*
- *Maintained relationships with people who reinforced my scarcity mindset*

Now it's time to get into the cost of what your Limiting Money Story has had on your life. The truth is we all want freedom. There is very common belief that "If I have all the money I wanted or needed, then my life would be perfect, happy, divine". The truth more often is our fear of being successful. Marianne Williamson says it best: "*Our deepest fear is not that we are inadequate. Our deepest fear is that we are powerful beyond measure. It is our light, not our darkness that most frightens us. We ask ourselves, 'Who am I to be brilliant, gorgeous, talented, fabulous?'"* So ask yourself "Who are you not?" Let's take a look at what not revealing your Inner Billionaire is costing you.

Calculating the Real Cost

Write down three opportunities you've passed up because of fear or doubt around money.

For each opportunity, ask yourself:
- What was the potential financial upside?
- What skills or connections might you have gained?
- How might your life be different today if you'd said yes?

Now, project forward five years:
- If you maintain your current beliefs about money, where will you be?
- What opportunities might you miss in the future?
- What's the cost of staying in this financial prison?

After you've done this sit in meditation for 10 minutes and integrate what you have uncovered about your Money Story. We will reflect on this later.

The Biology of Beliefs

Have you ever wondered why simply knowing you should think differently about money isn't enough to change your financial reality? I certainly did. I read every self-help book I could find, attended workshops, repeated affirmations – yet still found myself trapped in the same patterns. It wasn't until I understood how beliefs actually operate in our brains that real transformation became possible.

Think of your beliefs as neural highways in your brain. Every time you have a thought about money – whether it's "I'll never get ahead" or "There's never enough" – you're sending signals down specific neural pathways. The more you think these thoughts, the stronger these pathways become, just like a trail through a forest becomes more defined with repeated use.

I learned this lesson the hard way through my journey with addiction. Just as my brain had created powerful neural pathways around seeking substances, it had also built superhighways of scarcity thinking about money. Understanding this was crucial: these weren't character flaws or moral failings – they were literal physical patterns in my brain that could be rewired.

Everyday I watched clients live out their money stories daily. The single mom who believed against all odds that she could buy a home and did. The wealthy businessman who made millions but lived in constant fear of losing it all. The middle-class couple who kept sabotaging their loan approval because deep down, they didn't believe they deserved to upgrade their life.

Each of them was living proof of something profound: It's not our circumstances that create our financial reality - it's the stories we believe about what's possible for us.

Think about it. How many times have you heard about someone winning the lottery only to lose it all within a few years? Or someone starting from nothing and building an empire? Same circumstances, different stories, radically different outcomes.

This is why traditional financial advice so often fails. You can learn all the budgeting techniques in the world, read every money management book on the shelf, attend all the wealth seminars (trust me, I did) - but until you change your underlying story, nothing really changes.

I discovered this truth the hard way. No amount of financial knowledge could override my story about being bad at keeping money. No expert advice could trump my belief about the IRS debt being impossible to resolve. I had to change at a deeper level.

This is where our real work begins. In the next section, we're going to explore exactly how to rewrite your money story from the inside out. Not through force or positive thinking or willing yourself to believe something different - but through a profound shift in how you see yourself in relationship to abundance.

Because here's what I know for sure: Your current money story is just the first draft. And you, my friend, are about to become the conscious author of your financial future.

The moment you recognize your money story is just a story - not a life sentence - something profound shifts. It's like waking up from a dream and realizing you've been the Dreamweaver all along.

But before we can write a new story, we need to honor the old one. Yes, you heard me right. Those limiting beliefs, that scarcity mindset, that impossible IRS debt - they all served a purpose. My story of financial chaos protected me from something I was even more afraid of: truly owning my power.

What's your story protecting you from?

Let's find out together. Find a quiet space and a few minutes where you won't be interrupted, invite yourself to understand yourself more deeply.

Your Money Story Liberation Map

First, write down your current money story in all its messy glory. Don't edit, don't judge, just let it flow. Use what you uncovered in the previous section. (Mine started with "I'll always be in some kind of financial mess...")

Now, ask yourself these three questions:

1. How has this story kept me safe? (Example: "By believing I couldn't keep money, I never had to risk being truly successful...")
2. What has this story cost me? Example: "This story cost me years of freedom, peace of mind, and opportunities...")

3. What becomes possible when I release this story? Example: "Without this story, I could finally...")

Take your time with each question. Let the answers surprise you, be curious what comes up in from your inner wisdom's voice.

Here's what happened when I did this exercise: I realized my story about the IRS debt being impossible to resolve was actually protecting me from taking bold action. As long as it was "impossible," I didn't have to risk failing at solving it. Mind-blowing, right?

This understanding marked the beginning of my real transformation. Not because I immediately knew how to solve everything, but because I finally saw my story for what it was - a choice I could make differently.

As we close this chapter and prepare to step into the actual transformation process in Chapter 3, I want you to hold onto something powerful: Every limiting belief we've explored, every scarcity pattern we've uncovered, every money story we've identified - they're all just placeholder stories. They're the first draft, not the final version.

In the next chapter, we'll explore exactly how to write that new version. We'll dive into practical tools for healing your relationship with money, specific practices for embodying abundance, and the exact steps I took to transform my own financial reality.

But for now, just sit with your Story Liberation Map. Let yourself feel the possibility that's opening up. Because recognizing your current story is the first step to writing a new one.

And trust me, the story that's waiting to be written is far more magnificent than any limiting belief you've been carrying.

Ready to turn the page?

Chapter 3
HEALING YOUR MONEY WOUNDS

The Liberation Path

Ready to take your Story Liberation Map and write a new story? It's about to become your treasure map to freedom. But first, let me tell you what happened when I finally understood the difference between knowing my story and healing it.

I'd spent years in personal development, teaching others about abundance while secretly swimming in my own financial chaos. I could explain prosperity consciousness to anyone who'd listen. I could quote every spiritual teacher from Ernest Holmes to Eckhart Tolle. I knew all the right fundamental principles.

But here's what I finally understood: Knowing about healing is not the same as healing.

This hit home one day when I was leading a workshop on financial freedom. There I was, teaching others about abundance while my own IRS debt loomed over me like a storm cloud. The cognitive dissonance was exhausting. I knew what I "should" believe, how I "should" think, what I "should" do.

That's when I heard this quiet voice inside ask: "What if you stopped trying to fix yourself and started healing instead?"

The difference might sound subtle, but it was revolutionary. Fixing comes from a place of being broken. Healing comes from a place of becoming whole.

This is where most financial advice falls short. It tries to fix the symptoms- budgeting issues, debt, overspending - without healing the underlying wounds. It's like putting a band aid on a splinter without removing it first. The wound can't heal until you address what's really causing the pain.

Let me be clear: This chapter isn't about learning more financial strategies or positive thinking techniques. Those have their place, but they're not where true transformation begins. Instead, we're going to explore something much more powerful: how to heal your relationship with money at the deepest level.

Think of it this way: If your money story is the visible part of an iceberg, your money wounds are everything that lies beneath the surface. These wounds might come from:

- *Childhood experiences with lack or abundance*
- *Family patterns around wealth or poverty*
- *Societal messages about who gets to be wealthy*
- *Personal traumas involving money*
- *Spiritual beliefs about prosperity*

In my case, the wounds ran deep. Yes, there was the obvious trauma of massive debt, but beneath that lay older wounds: watching my father's financial chaos, absorbing my mother's Depression-era fears, believing I had to struggle to be worthy.

These wounds weren't healed by learning better money management (though that helped). They weren't healed by positive affirmations (though I tried those too). They were healed through a process of deep, honest recognition and release.

Before we go further, let's pause for a moment. Take a deep breath. Place one hand on your heart and one on your belly. Feel the wisdom that lives in your body, the healing that's already beginning, the abundance that's always been yours.

This is where our real journey begins - not in fixing what's broken, but in remembering what's whole. Throughout this chapter, we'll explore practical tools for healing your money wounds, but we'll do it from this place of wholeness, not brokenness.

Your transformation isn't about becoming someone new. It's about releasing what stands between you and who you've always been.

Are you ready to begin?

I have a shelf full of financial self-help books. You know the ones - how to budget, how to invest, how to think and grow rich. I'd attend every wealth seminar I could find, frantically taking notes about money management strategies and investment techniques. I even became an expert at teaching others about financial success.

Yet there I was, successful on paper but still creating financial chaos in my personal life.

Here's what nobody tells you: Traditional financial advice is like trying to heal a broken heart by learning how to date better. Sure, the techniques might be useful, but they're not addressing the real issue.

Think about it. Most financial advice focuses on three things:

1. Budgeting better
2. Earning more
3. Investing wisely

All valuable skills. But they're like trying to sail a boat without first untying it from the dock. You can hoist the best sails, plot the perfect course, even hire an expert crew - but if you're still anchored to old wounds and limiting beliefs, you're not going anywhere.

I watched this play out countless times with clients. I'd help them create solid financial plans for homeownership, creating businesses, investment or debt relief. We'd structure everything perfectly on paper. But then something interesting would happen:

Some clients would sail smoothly toward their goals, while others would mysteriously self-sabotage at the last minute. Same advice, same strategies, dramatically different results. Why?

Because financial advice that doesn't address the body-mind connection is missing the most crucial piece of the puzzle: You can't think your way out of trauma that lives in your body.

Let me say that again: You can't think your way out of trauma that lives in your body.

I learned this truth the hard way. All my knowledge about finance couldn't override my body's ingrained response to money situations. My nervous system was programmed for financial chaos long before I learned about budgeting.

When I'd receive a large commission check, my body would literally go into fight-or-flight mode despite what you might imagine would happen when someone "receives money." My breathing would get shallow. My shoulders would tense. My stomach would knot up. Before I'd even made a conscious decision, my body was already executing its familiar pattern of spend-avoid-crash.

This is why a simple desire, or "willpower", doesn't work long-term. Willpower is a conscious mind. Trauma is body memory. And in any contest between mind and body, body wins. **Every time!**

Think about the last time you tried to follow traditional financial advice. Maybe it was creating a budget, starting a savings plan, or investing for the future. How did your body feel? Did you experience:

Tightness in your chest?
Shallow breathing?
Stomach tension?
Nervous energy?
An urge to avoid or escape?

These aren't character flaws or lack of discipline. They're your body's programmed responses to money situations. And until we address these physical patterns, no amount of financial knowledge will create lasting change.

Here's what I have come to KNOW: Real financial transformation begins with healing the body's relationship with money. This means:

Understanding your nervous system's money patterns.

Releasing stored financial trauma from your body
Creating new somatic (body-based) responses to money situations
Building physical confidence with wealth

This isn't woo-woo stuff - it's neuroscience. Your body keeps score of every financial experience you've ever had, every money message you've ever received, every scarcity story you've ever believed. That score is held in your muscles, your breathing patterns, your nervous system responses.

The good news? Just as your body learned these patterns, it can learn new ones. But not through spreadsheets, budgets or even business strategies alone. We need a whole new approach - one that honors the body's wisdom while creating new pathways for abundance.

That's exactly what we're going to explore next: the profound connection between your body and your financial reality, and how to begin transforming both together.

But first, I invite you to do something radical: Thank all those financial books and seminars for getting you this far. They served a purpose. They gave you valuable tools. AND they weren't designed to heal the deeper patterns we're about to address.

You're not failing at financial advice. Financial advice has failed to address what you really need: whole-person healing that includes your body, mind, and spirit.

Are you ready to discover what becomes possible when you bring your whole self to financial transformation?

The Mind Body Connection in Financial Healing

The first time I experienced a profound body-mind shift around money, I was sitting in a trauma therapy session. I hadn't come to discuss finances- I was there to work through my addiction recovery. But as we explored my patterns, something unexpected emerged: every time we touched on money topics, my entire body would contract.

"Notice that," my coach said. "Your shoulders just hunched, your breathing got shallow, and you're literally trying to make yourself smaller. What's happening in your body right now?"

I realized I was physically bracing for impact - as if money itself was a threat to my survival. This wasn't a conscious thought. It was a deeply programmed bodily response, one that had been running my financial life without my awareness.

This is what we need to understand about money trauma: it lives in our nervous system. Every financial panic, every scarcity experience, every money-related fear gets stored in our bodies. Your muscles remember the tension of checking your bank balance. Your breath holds the pattern of financial anxiety. Your gut carries the imprint of every money crisis, lack experience and imprinting of money patterns.

Take a moment right now and check in with your body. Notice how it responds to money in general and financial experiences you've had:

- When you check your accounts
- When you need to pay bills
- When unexpected expenses arise
- When money conversations come up
- When opportunities for wealth appear

Begin to notice and become aware of:

- Your breathing patterns
- Muscle tension
- Stomach sensations
- Energy levels
- Fight/flight/freeze responses

These physical responses aren't random - they're programmed reactions based on past experiences. And here's what's crucial to understand: These bodily responses happen faster than thought. Before your conscious mind can even process a financial situation, your body is already executing its protective patterns.

I saw this clearly in my own life. Even after I understood my limiting beliefs about money, even after I could teach others about abundance, my body would still react with panic to certain financial situations. It wasn't until I began working with this body-mind connection that real transformation became possible.

Here's what I discovered: Our bodies carry three distinct layers of financial programming:

1. Survival Patterns
These are our most primitive money responses - the fight/flight/freeze reactions to financial stress. Mine showed up as freezing when bills arrived, even when I had plenty of money to pay them.

2. Emotional Imprints
These are the feelings we've associated with money - shame, fear, excitement, unworthiness. I carried the physical sensation of "not enough" in my chest, a constant tightness that no amount of money could relax.

3. Identity Embodiment
This is how our bodies literally shape themselves around our money story. I used to physically shrink myself in wealthy environments, unconsciously trying to become invisible.

Understanding these layers is crucial because each requires a different healing approach. You can't talk yourself out of a survival response. You can't budget your way through emotional trauma. You can't positive-think your way into new embodiment.

Let me show you what this means practically. When I was facing that massive IRS debt, my typical pattern would be:

> Survival Response: Freeze and avoid
> Emotional Imprint: Overwhelming shame
> Identity Embodiment: Making myself small

Traditional financial advice would tell me to face my fears and make a payment plan. But my body wasn't having it. Every time I tried to take action, my nervous system would shut down in panic.

Real transformation began when I started working with my body instead of against it. This meant:

1. Calming my survival responses through breath work
2. Releasing emotional trauma through somatic practices
3. Creating new embodiment patterns through movement

The results were profound. As my body began to feel safe with money, my external financial reality started shifting too. Solutions appeared that I couldn't see before. Opportunities emerged that my panic-driven system would have previously rejected.

This is what holistic financial healing looks like - working with both body and mind together. In the next section, we'll explore specific somatic practices that can begin shifting your body's relationship with money.

But first, let's do a quick body awareness check:

Take a deep breath, place your left hand on your heart and right hand on your abdomen and ask your body:

- Where does money live in my body?
- What sensations arise when I think about wealth?
- Where do I feel financial tension?
- What parts of me relax when thinking about abundance?

Just notice. Don't try to change anything yet. The awareness itself begins the healing process.

Remember: Your body isn't your enemy in financial transformation - it's your most powerful ally. Once we understand how to work with our body's wisdom instead of against its protective patterns, we open the door to profound change.

That's exactly what we'll explore next - specific practices for creating this transformation.

Somatic Practices for Financial Transformation

When I first learned about somatic practices for healing my relationship with money, I was skeptical. First a quick understanding of Somatic Practices. Simply put Somatic practices are body-centered techniques designed to enhance awareness of the mind-body connection. In your financial transformation they foster emotional awareness. If all your emotions are stored in the body, it's a logical next step to begin to become aware of how your body responds to your financial stories.

So here's truth. The most practical solution is the one that actually works. And for deep-seated money patterns, that means starting with the body.

Let me share the three most powerful somatic practices that transformed my financial reality and hundreds of my clients.

The Money Breath
I noticed I was literally holding my breath around money - when checking accounts, paying bills, even receiving payments. This chronic breath-holding was keeping my nervous system in a constant state of financial panic.

Here's the practice that changed everything:

Sit comfortably and place one hand on your belly. Imagine your wealth flowing like a river. As you inhale, feel your belly expand as you receive abundance. As you exhale, feel yourself releasing financial tension. Start with three minutes daily, especially before any money activities.

What happened when I practiced this consistently? My nervous system began to associate money with breathing, with life force, with flow. Financial decisions became easier because my body wasn't in constant panic mode.

The Abundance Stance
Our posture literally shapes our relationship with wealth. I used to physically collapse around money, making myself smaller in financial situations. Begin to

notice your posture. Do you make yourself smaller, hunch over, round your shoulders, create a stuck energy in your body?

Here is a perfect way to become aware:

Stand as if you're completely wealthy. Notice what changes in your:

> Spine alignment
> Shoulder position
> Head carriage
> Facial expression
> Overall energy

Now hold this "wealthy" posture while doing money tasks. Pay bills from this stance. Check accounts from this position. Make financial decisions from this embodiment.

The Power of Movement

Money stagnation often reflects physical stagnation. When I felt financially stuck, my body was literally frozen in protective patterns.

This practice transformed that:

You can create a personal "money movement"-a way of physically expressing your relationship with wealth. It might be:

> *A prosperity dance*
> *A wealth walk*
> *An abundance stretch*
> *A success spin*

The key is making it yours. My money movement became a spiraling dance that helped me feel abundance flowing through every cell.

But here's what's crucial: These aren't just exercises - they're ways of reprogramming your nervous system's relationship with money. Practice them consistently, especially:

- Before financial decisions
- During money conversations
- When receiving income
- While paying bills
- When feeling financially triggered

Remember: Your body learns through repetition. Each time you practice these somatic tools, you're creating new neural pathways for wealth.

Let me show you how this worked practically. When facing any challenging financial situation, I would:

1. Start with Money Breath to calm my nervous system
2. Move into Abundance Stance to access my power
3. Do my Money Movement to release stagnation
4. Then take practical action from this embodied state

The results? Solutions I couldn't see before became visible. My body stopped fighting wealth. Financial decisions became clearer because I wasn't operating from panic.

A crucial note: This isn't about forcing your body to feel something it doesn't. It's about creating safe spaces for your nervous system to explore new possibilities with money.

Start small. Maybe just ten conscious breaths while checking your bank balance. Perhaps thirty seconds of standing in your power before paying bills. A brief movement practice when feeling financially contracted.

Your body will tell you what it needs. Trust that wisdom. Notice:

> *What practices feel nurturing?*
> *Where does your system need more support?*
> *What movements create more financial flow?*
> *How does your breath change with different practices?*

Every financial pattern you have was learned by your body. That means your body can learn new patterns. These somatic practices are your tools for that rewiring.

In our next section, we'll explore how to strengthen these new patterns by creating fresh neural pathways. But for now, just experiment with one somatic practice that calls to you. Let your body lead the way to transformation.

Creating New Neuropathways for Wealth

The brain science behind my financial transformation fascinated me. Here I was, teaching myself new money behaviors, and somewhere in my brain, actual physical changes were happening. Neural pathways - those information highways in our brains - were being redirected from scarcity to abundance. This wasn't just spiritual principles at work, but scientific as well.

Think of it like this: Every time you have a thought or experience about money, you're creating a pathway in your brain. Do it enough times, and that pathway becomes like a well-worn trail through a forest. My scarcity trail was practically a superhighway after years of use.

But here's the amazing thing about neural plasticity (the ability of your brain to create new behaviors), we can create new pathways at any time. AT ANY TIME! Right now as you read these words your mind is rewiring.

I discovered this truth while creating the wealth to pay off the IRS lien. Every time I responded differently to a financial trigger, I was literally carving a new trail in my brain. Instead of following my usual panic pathway, I was creating an alternative route, one of abundance, freedom and confidence.

Here's how you build these new neural pathways:

The 90-Second Reset
When a financial trigger hits:

1. Notice the old pathway activating (racing heart, tight chest, panic thoughts)
2. Pause for 90 seconds - this is how long it takes for stress chemicals to flush from your system
3. Consciously choose a new response

I used this practice every time I opened mail from the IRS. Instead of diving into panic, I'd, notice my stress response, wait 90 second while breathing deeply THEN and only then would I approach the situation with my new abundance pathway. You have to calm your body first in order to create new neuropathways.

The Wealth Visualization Circuit
The concept that "your brain does not know the difference between a vividly imagined experience and a "real one" is rooted in the principles of hypnosis, meditation and visualization. I learned this as a practicing hypnotherapist. Research of quantum physics and neuroscience now evidence that your brain becomes receptive to suggestions and imagery in a deep meditation state. Our brains are mystical and magical on so many levels. In a deep meditative state your brain processes imagined scenarios in the same way it does "real" experiences, thereby activating the same neural pathways. This is why visualization techniques can be powerful for manifesting your desires. By repeatedly exposing your brain to vivid mental images you can effectively "program" your subconscious mind to believe this reality.

In a nutshell, your brain can't tell the difference between a vividly imagined experience and a real one.

How can you use this to your advantage? With simply daily practices such as these:

Sit quietly for five minutes
Imagine in detail handling money confidently
Feel the physical sensations of financial ease
Engage all your senses in this new reality

Key point: Do this when you're calm, not in financial stress.

You're creating the pathway before you need it.

Pattern Interruption

One of Tony Robbins favorite methodologies is to "break your state". He tells a story of coaching a client in his early days and the client was in a loop telling the same story over and over. Tony finally threw a glass of water in his face. What this illustrates is sometimes we have to "pattern interrupt" our habitual programming. You may not have to throw water in your own face, but here are some ideas to break habitual money responses:

- Use your non-dominant hand to pay bills
- Take a different route to the bank
- Change your bill-paying environment
- Create new money rituals

These are just forms of interruption in order to create an opportunity for new neural wiring. The crucial element? Consistency. Neural pathways strengthen through repetition. I practiced these techniques daily, especially when I didn't feel like it.

Results emerged gradually, then suddenly. One day I realized I was handling financial situations with a calm I'd never known before. The new pathways had become my default routes. Your brain will always choose the most familiar path. Our job is making abundance responses more familiar than scarcity, fear, lack reactions.

Start small. Choose one financial situation that typically triggers you. Apply these techniques just to that scenario. As the new pathway strengthens, expand to other areas. Your brain is rewiring itself right now, just by engaging with these concepts. Every conscious choice to respond differently to money creates another step on your new abundance trail.

Next, we'll explore how to reinforce these new pathways through conscious relationship with money - starting with the revolutionary practice of the Money Date.

The Money Date – Building Conscious Relationship with Wealth

Money is the most important relationship you will ever have in your life. And before you say your spouse, kids, parents, siblings are, hear me out. Money is how you experience and express your worthiness. You depend on it for food, clothing, shelter and a host of survival and pleasure. I learned years ago that feeling into money as your most important partner relationship, you begin to see how life is truly abundant. Imagine money is the most incredible life partner of your dreams. How would the perfect partner treat you? In a perfect scenario, like a Queen, a precious being, providing your wants and needs unconditionally. Instead what I see are people treat money like you would a partner you don't trust and might even be ready to break up with. Would you ignore your partner for months, only checking in when there's a crisis? Constantly condemn it for causing chaos in your life. Be jealous that it blesses others more than you? Hide from it, ignore it, resent it? Yet that's exactly how most of us treat our relationship with money.

Enter the **Money Date** - a practice that transformed my entire financial reality.

The first time I sat down for an intentional Money Date, I felt ridiculous. There I was, lighting candles, playing soft music, preparing to... look at my bank statements? But something magical happened when I approached money with the same care and attention, I'd give to nurturing an important relationship. Money is just a form of energy and loves to be treated as the great love of your life. So if you begin to hold it in esteem, not as a power over you but a loving, giving respectful relationship transformation is imminent. How to begin to foster that relationship? A Money Date!

Here's how to create your own Money Date:

Set the Scene
Choose a regular time (weekly works best)
Create a beautiful environment
Remove distractions
Bring your favorite beverage
Light a candle or play music that makes you feel abundant

The Date Structure:

1. Gratitude Opening
- Acknowledge recent financial blessings
- Celebrate any money wins, no matter how small
- Express appreciation for money's presence in your life

2. Present Moment Check-in
- Review current financial status without judgment
- Notice your body's response to different accounts/numbers
- Practice your somatic tools if tension arises

3. Future Vision
- Dream about your next financial steps
- Visualize your expanding abundance
- Make empowered choices about upcoming money moves

4. Closing Ritual
- Thank money for its presence
- Set clear intentions for the week ahead
- End with a gesture of appreciation (I blow out the candle)

The key? Consistency over perfection. My early Money Dates were awkward, emotional, sometimes tearful. But each one built trust - both with money and with myself.

This practice helped me face my IRS situation with new eyes. Instead of avoiding financial reality, I created a safe space to engage with it. Solutions emerged not from panic, but from partnership.

Your Money Date is sacred time. Protect it like you would any important relationship. Because that's exactly what it is - you're building a conscious, loving relationship with wealth itself, with the abundant nature of the universe.

Start with just 15 minutes. Notice what shifts when you treat money as a welcomed guest rather than an avoided enemy. Watch how your financial reality transforms when you give it this kind of consistent, loving attention.

Remember: This isn't about getting the numbers perfect. It's about creating a new relationship with the energy of money itself.

Building Trust with Abundance

Trust is earned in drops and lost in buckets. This was especially true in my relationship with money. Each time I made and broke a financial promise to myself, I eroded that precious trust. Each time I avoided looking at my accounts or dodged money conversations, the trust gap widened.

Building trust with abundance is like rehabilitating any damaged relationship - it happens through small, consistent actions over time.

Start with Tiny Promises like these:

> *Promise yourself to check one account today*
> *Commit to opening every bill when it arrives*
> *Pledge to track one day's spending*

Then keep those promises. No matter what.

I started with just opening IRS notices and all bills immediately instead of avoiding them. This small act of courage began rebuilding my trust muscle. Each time I kept a financial promise to myself, I proved I was trustworthy.

Create Safety Rituals

Your nervous system needs to feel safe with wealth. Here are a few ways you can begin to create that peace and harmony with your nervous system:

> *Hold cash while doing deep breathing*
> *Practice receiving compliments about money*
> *Celebrate every financial win, no matter how small*
> *Thank money when it flows out, not just when it comes in*

My ritual became counting cash slowly each morning while breathing deeply. This simple practice helped my body associate money with safety instead of panic.

Track Your Trust Growth

Begin to keep a "Trust Evidence Journal":

> *Note every kept financial promise*
> *Record abundance synchronicities*
> *Document money "miracles"*
> *Celebrate your progress*

This isn't about toxic positivity - it's about training your brain to notice evidence of trustworthiness.

Most importantly: Trust takes time. Don't rush this process. Each small step builds the foundation for lasting transformation.

You're not just building trust with money - you're rebuilding trust with yourself as a steward of abundance.

Daily Practices for Lasting Transformation

The deepest shifts happen in daily moments, not dramatic breakthroughs. After facing my mountains of debt and transforming my money story, I discovered that sustained abundance requires consistent practice. Like tending a garden, financial freedom needs daily nurturing.

Here's your Daily Abundance Practice Blueprint
Morning Practice (10 minutes):

- Money Breath: 3 minutes of conscious breathing
- Abundance Embodiment: Stand in your wealth posture
- Gratitude: Note 3 specific financial blessings
- Intention: Set one clear money intention for the day

Throughout Day:
- Pattern Interruption: Notice and redirect scarcity thoughts
- Somatic Check-ins: Brief body awareness moments
- Conscious Language: Use abundance vocabulary
- Celebration: Acknowledge all money flows, in and out

Evening Practice (5 minutes):
- Trust Evidence: Record kept financial promises
- Progress Notes: Document abundance manifestations
- Next-Day Setup: Prepare for tomorrow's money activities

Weekly Anchors:

- Money Date: Sacred time with your finances
- Neural Pathway Review: Track new abundance habits
- Somatic Integration: Deeper body-based practices
- Trust Building: Review and strengthen financial promises

This isn't about perfection. It's about consistent, loving attention to your relationship with abundance. Start with one practice that resonates. Add others as they feel natural.

Create your own Sacred Money Rituals
- A prosperity altar in your home
- Monthly abundance ceremonies
- Seasonal financial reviews
- Wealth manifestation practices

Your Financial Liberation Contract
Finally it's time to make a commitment to yourself, not to me or anyone else, but yourself about your decision to embrace abundance, prosperity and trust. If you are ready to make that commitment, hand write this in your journal.

I, _____, commit to:

Honoring my body's wisdom about money
Building trust with abundance daily
Keeping small promises to myself
Celebrating all financial flows
Creating new neural pathways for wealth

Sign and date this contract. Place it where you'll see it daily. Let it remind you of your commitment to conscious partnership with abundance.

The journey we've explored - from understanding money wounds to healing them through body-based practices - is ongoing. Each day brings new opportunities to choose abundance over scarcity, trust over fear, conscious partnership over unconscious patterns.

Your transformation is already happening. Every breath, every choice, every moment of awareness is rewiring your relationship with wealth. Trust this process. Trust yourself. Trust the abundance that's always been yours.

Welcome to your new financial reality. The practice begins now.

Chapter 4

THE SCIENCE AND FOUNDATION OF GRATITUDE

Why Your Brain Loves to Say Thank You

Picture this: It's 3 AM in the cancer ward, and I'm counting IV drops like they're chocolate chips in my mom's baking cabinet. Everything I used to think meant wealth - my businesses, my manifesting mojo, my material success - seemed about as meaningful as a counterfeit hundred in a strip club. Yet there I was, having what can only be described as a gratitude epiphany while high on legal drugs (a refreshing change from my usual chemical adventures).

The nurse came in to adjust my medication, her movements gentle and practiced. In my morphine-enhanced state, I started noticing things: the sophisticated equipment keeping me alive, the sterile environment that some poor soul had to maintain at 3 AM, the skilled staff who chose night shift instead of normal-people hours. My analytical mind - the same one that used to calculate how many rocks I could buy with a commission check - began cataloging these blessings like I was taking inventory at a gratitude warehouse.

What I didn't know then (because hey, who reads neuroscience journals during radiation?) was that my brain was doing something extraordinary. That simple act of noticing and appreciating was literally rewiring my neural circuitry. This wasn't just positive thinking or some prosperity gospel pitch - this was hardcore science having a party in my prefrontal cortex.

Now, before you start thinking this is going to be some dry scientific lecture (though I do love to geek out harder than a Star Trek convention about how our brains work), let me tell you why this matters to your bank account, your healing, and yes, even your love life.

The Science Behind Why Gratitude Works

How Your Brain Gets High on Thank You

I could manifest six-figure deals during my drug addicted days. Why? Well, turns out there's actually a scientific explanation for why I could pull that off (besides being higher than a SpaceX rocket). When we feel genuine gratitude, our brains undergo changes that make us better at spotting opportunities than a drug dealer at a police convention.

The folks at UC Davis (who probably never imagined their research would be explained using drug dealer metaphors) found that just 21 days of consistent gratitude practice increases your ability to spot abundance by 25%. That's right - being thankful makes you better at noticing good stuff than a chocolate addict in a Godiva store.

But here's where it gets really interesting. The HeartMath Institute (which sounds like a Valentine's Day factory but is actually a serious research facility) discovered that when we practice genuine gratitude, our heart's electromagnetic field expands up to 60 times its normal size. That's like your heart going from a studio apartment to a mansion with an ocean view.

The Biology of Blessing

How Your Body Gets High on Gratitude

Let me tell you about the vagus nerve - it's like your body's information superhighway, except instead of carrying cat videos and spam emails, it carries messages between your brain and body. During my cancer treatment, I noticed something wild: on days when I managed to feel grateful (even for small things like not having hospital Jell-O for lunch), my body actually responded better to treatment. The nurses thought I was just being a model patient, but nope - I was accidentally doing science.

You see, when we activate gratitude, our bodies start producing stuff that makes pharmaceutical companies jealous. Natural killer cells increase (which sounds terrifying but is actually awesome), immunoglobulin A goes up (fancy word for "stuff that fights infection"), and inflammation goes down faster than my bank balance in my using days.

But here's the kicker - these changes happen faster than you can say "thank you." Dr. Rollin McCraty (yes, that's his real name, and yes, I'm jealous I didn't think of it first) proved that heartfelt appreciation creates immediate positive changes in your body. It's like hitting the biological lottery, except instead of buying a ticket, you just need to feel grateful.

The Quantum Connection

How Being Thankful Bends Reality

Now, let's get really weird. Remember in my mortgage days when I understood spreadsheets and closing costs? Well, quantum physics makes that look like kindergarten math. Stay with me here, because this is where it gets good.

Quantum physics shows that just observing something changes it. It's like when you're looking for your keys - the moment you stop searching and say "thank you for showing up," boom, there they are on the coffee table where you've already looked twelve times. This isn't coincidence; it's science (though it probably won't hold up as an excuse for being late to work).

During my IRS negotiations, instead of obsessing over the impossibility of my situation (which, let's face it, was about as likely as finding a vegetarian at a Texas BBQ), I started practicing deliberate gratitude for any tiny movement forward. Suddenly, solutions started popping up like mushrooms after rain. People who could help appeared out of nowhere, like my own personal abundance flash mob.

The Body-Mind Bridge

How Your Cells Party on Gratitude

The day I discovered my body was keeping score of my gratitude level was like finding out my ex was tracking my Instagram - both fascinating and slightly unnerving. During a financial therapy session (yes, that's a thing, and yes, I needed it), my teacher asked me to notice what happened in my body when I thought about money. My shoulders immediately tensed up like I was preparing to bench press my IRS debt.

This is what science calls the body-mind bridge, though I prefer to think of it as your internal abundance GPS. When you're genuinely grateful, your body creates what scientists call an "upward spiral" - which is basically like your cells doing the happy dance.

Let me show you how this works in real life. During my recovery from both addiction and cancer (because apparently, I like to overachieve even in my struggles), I developed what I call "gratitude anchors." Instead of reaching for a pipe or a pill when stress hit, I'd put my hand on my heart for financial decisions, take deep belly breaths while paying, and practice gentle movement for abundance meditation.

The Quantum Dance of Gratitude

Getting Your Atoms to Party with Abundance

Let's dive deeper into this quantum weirdness. During my research phase (which happened mostly at 3 AM in the hospital when the good drugs kicked in), I discovered something mind-bending from Princeton's PEAR laboratories.

These folks spent years proving that human consciousness directly influences physical reality at the quantum level. In other words, your "thank yous" are literally rearranging atoms.

Think about that for a second. When I was manifesting mortgage deals during my addiction days, I wasn't just getting lucky - I was actually bending reality. The problem was, I was also programming that same reality for loss because my gratitude had more holes than a crack pipe.

Dr. William Tiller (who sounds like he should be farming but actually studies quantum physics) proved that focused appreciation changes the quantum field around us. It's like your gratitude creates a ripple effect in the universe, except instead of ripples in a pond, you're creating waves in the fabric of reality itself.

During my darkest times - and let's face it, smoking crack while owing the IRS enough money to buy a small island definitely qualifies as dark - I learned to find genuine gratitude for tiny things. A warm shower. A safe place to sleep. The fact that my dealer had reliable business hours (okay, maybe not that last one). Each authentic "thank you" was literally rewiring the quantum field around me.

Your Body's Abundance Antenna

How Your Cells Tune into the Prosperity Channel

Remember my financial therapy session? Well, it turns out my body wasn't just being dramatic about money - it was actually running a sophisticated feedback system that would make NASA jealous. Dr. Stephen Porges (another scientist with a cool name) discovered that our nervous system has three main states

1. Freeze - Think possum playing dead or me when the IRS letters arrived
2. Fight/Flight - My default setting during tax season
3. Social Engagement - The sweet spot where abundance flows

The trick is getting your body from panic mode into that prosperity-receiving zone. It's like trying to tune an old radio - you have to fiddle with the dial just right to get rid of the static and hear the music clearly.

Here's what I developed during my recovery that I call "The Gratitude Reset" (patent pending, just kidding):

First, notice where you're holding tension. During my debt days, I carried so much stress in my shoulders I could've been mistaken for a bodybuilder. Take a moment to consciously soften those areas - yes, even your jaw (I know you're clenching it right now).

Then, create some physical comfort. Maybe it's wrapping yourself in a cozy blanket, or in my case, finally letting myself enjoy those fancy hospital sheets instead of feeling guilty about the thread count.

Now, here's where the magic happens - allow appreciation to bubble up naturally. Don't force it like you're trying to squeeze the last bit of toothpaste out of the tube. Just let it come, like remembering lyrics to a song you haven't heard in years.

The Evidence Lab

Turning Your Life into a Gratitude Science Experiment

During my financial recovery (which sounds much fancier than "trying not to go broke again"), I decided to treat my life like a laboratory. I started tracking gratitude outcomes.

Every morning, I'd note my heart rate, energy level, and what I call my "gratitude state" (ranging from "grumpy cat" to "Dalai Lama"). Every evening, I'd record any "coincidences" (spoiler alert: there's no such thing), opportunity flows, and what I call "manifestation moments."

After 30 days, the results were clearer than a drug test I would have failed spectacularly in my previous life:

- My stress dropped faster than my morals during active addiction
- Opportunities started showing up like groupies at a rock concert
- "Lucky" coincidences multiplied like rabbits on fertility drugs
- Money started flowing in ways that made my accountant dizzy

But here's what really blew my mind - something the research hadn't predicted. As I worked with gratitude as a science, it started feeling less like an experiment and more like a sacred practice. It was like discovering that your favorite dance moves actually burn calories - the fun part was the point all along, the benefits were just bonus.

The Sacred Science Sweet Spot

Where Einstein Meets Enlightenment

So here's what blows my mind more than any research paper or clinical study: While science proves gratitude's power (in ways that would make my old drug tests look amateur), the real magic happens in that sweet spot where data meets divine, where metrics kiss mystery.

Think about it like music. My Grammie's piano taught me that understanding music theory can make you technically proficient - knowing all the scales and keys is great. But add soul to that knowledge? Now you're creating art that makes people cry in a good way.

During my healing journey - from addiction, from cancer, from crushing debt - I learned to play both parts: the meticulous researcher tracking results and the spiritual seeker following the heart's wisdom. It's like being a DJ at the universe's greatest party, mixing the scientific beat with the soul's melody.

And that's where our next chapter begins. We're about to explore what happens when we take all this juicy science - the neural pathways, the quantum physics, the biological transformations - and let it dance with something even more powerful: the sacred art of grateful living.

Your Inner Billionaire

Think you're ready to let your inner scientist waltz with your inner mystic? Let's dive in...

Chapter 5

BUILDING YOUR ABUNDANCE FOUNDATION

The Gratitude Gateway

So there I was, on my porch at 4 AM, having what can only be described as an existential crisis with a side of insomnia. After spending weeks geeking out about neural pathways and quantum physics (which, let's face it, is more fun than it should be when you're on good intravenous morphine), I found myself watching the sky do its daily magic show.

You know that moment just before dawn when the whole world seems to hold its breath? In that sacred pause between night and day, magic happens. On one such morning, as I watched the sky slowly illuminate, something profound shifted. The same sun that had risen billions of times before was creating something entirely new. In that moment, I understood - abundance isn't something we chase or achieve. It's something we open to receive, like the earth receiving daylight.

Sitting on my porch swing at 4 AM, unable to sleep from worry about financial overwhelm. What began as insomnia became my gateway to understanding true wealth. When even the birds are like "five more minutes, please"? That's when it hit me - harder than an IRS audit letter but way more pleasant. All this science we've been exploring, all these studies about gratitude rewiring our brains and restructuring our reality, they're just the tip of the cosmic iceberg.

Think about it: That same sun that was about to make its appearance had been doing this dance billions of times before I decided to have my enlightenment moment on a secondhand porch swing. Yet every single sunrise is completely new, utterly unique, like a divine artist who never runs out of inspiration.

This wasn't just sleep deprivation talking (though I'll admit, those 4 AM insights can be questionable). This was the moment when all that delicious science we discussed in the previous chapter, started doing the cha-cha-cha with something deeper, something sacred. It was like the researcher in me finally asked the mystic out for coffee, and they really hit it off.

Here's what I understood sitting there, watching night surrender to day: Abundance isn't something we chase like I used to chase my next fix. It's something we open to receive, like the earth receiving daylight. No striving, no struggling, just a natural unfolding.

Sure, we can measure the chemical changes in our brains when we practice gratitude (and isn't it cool that we can?). We can track how our nervous system shifts from "panic in the tax office" mode to "abundance receiving" mode. But there's something else happening too - something that can't be graphed or measured or put in a PowerPoint presentation.

We spent the last chapter understanding the science of gratitude - how it changes our brain chemistry, alters our nervous system, and creates measurable transformation. Now we'll explore something equally powerful but less quantifiable: how gratitude becomes a sacred gateway to abundance.

Think of gratitude like breathing. Yes, there's complex biology involved - oxygen exchange, cellular respiration, autonomic nervous system regulation. But there's also the sacred experience of that first breath at birth, the last breath at death, and all the conscious breaths in between that connect us to life itself.

This is the feminine energy of gratitude - not as a practice to perfect, but as a sacred dance to embody. It's less about counting blessings and more about becoming the blessing. Less about manifesting abundance and more about recognizing we are abundance incarnate.

I remember the exact moment this understanding landed in my bones. I was sitting in a surgeon's office waiting to hear if I would have to wear a colostomy bag the rest of my life, feeling perhaps the furthest from abundance I'd ever felt. My business was gone, my savings depleted, my body failing. Yet as I watched the sunrise through the hospital window, something in me recognized: Even here, even now, I am wealth itself.

This isn't about positive thinking or spiritual bypassing. This is about accessing the deepest truth of who we are - beings made of the same stuff as stars, inherently abundant simply because we exist. When we tap into this truth through sacred gratitude, we open gateways that no external circumstance can close.

Let me show you how to access this gateway - not through striving or struggling, but through surrender into the sacred. Your abundance isn't waiting in some distant future. It's waiting in the temple of your own heart, and gratitude holds the key.

Welcome to the sacred art of grateful living. Let's begin...

Finding Gratitude in Dark Times

Christmas morning, 1992, I sat alone in my apartment, eating cookies and drinking milk from the dollar store. My family had essentially excommunicated me that year because of my addiction. By any external measure, this was rock bottom. Yet in that moment of complete aloneness, I discovered something extraordinary - gratitude doesn't require ideal circumstances. Sometimes our deepest appreciation emerges from our darkest places.

The cookies weren't gourmet. The milk wasn't organic. But as I sat there, something shifted. I began to notice things - the quiet of the morning, the way sunlight played on my wall, the simple sweetness of sugar cookies. In the midst of what should have been devastating loneliness, I found myself experiencing a peculiar kind of peace.

This is what I've come to understand about sacred gratitude - it's not about waiting for perfect conditions. It's about finding the holy in the humble, the divine in the difficult, the sacred in the simple.

Let me share another gateway moment. I was lying in my hospital bed during radiation treatment, feeling stripped of everything that had once defined my success - my thriving businesses, my financial stability, my physical vitality. The hospital gown had replaced my power suits. The medical bills had replaced my commission checks. Yet in that space of supreme surrender, something profound awakened.

I began to notice the small graces, the gentle way my nurse adjusted my pillows, the warmth of sunlight through my window, the steady rhythm of my own breath and the card from friends I never expected to care.

Each of these became a doorway to deeper gratitude. Not the superficial "think positive" kind, but the soul-deep recognition that even here, even now, grace was present.

This is what transforms gratitude from a practice into a portal - when we stop trying to be grateful for what we think we should appreciate and start discovering what's genuinely touching our hearts in each moment.

During my tax lien crisis, when I owed more money than I could imagine paying in several lifetimes, I discovered that gratitude could exist alongside fear. I didn't have to wait until the debt was resolved to find things to appreciate. In fact, it was my willingness to be grateful even while terrified that began shifting the entire situation.

Each morning, I would:
Light a candle
Place one hand on my heart
Breathe deeply
Find one genuine thing to appreciate

Some days it was just "Thank you for another chance to try." Other days it was gratitude for a supportive phone call or an unexpected lead. The size of the appreciation didn't matter - its authenticity did.

This is the sacred feminine way - finding beauty not despite our wounds but through them. Like the Japanese art of Kintsugi, where broken pottery is mended with gold, our darkest experiences become luminous when infused with genuine gratitude.

Let me be clear - this isn't about denying difficulty or pretending everything is fine. It's about developing the capacity to hold both: the challenge and the blessing, the pain and the beauty, the fear and the appreciation. This is mature gratitude - not the glossy surface kind, but the deep, soul-nourishing variety that can transform our darkest moments into doorways of grace.

The Natural Rhythms of Gratitude

Nature never forces the changing of seasons. The moon doesn't strain to complete its cycle. Each phase flows naturally into the next, creating a perfect dance of expansion and contraction. During my healing journey, I discovered this same natural rhythm within gratitude itself.

I remember the exact moment this understanding dawned. It was a new moon night during my cancer treatment, and I was feeling particularly low. Instead of forcing myself to write my usual gratitude list, I just sat in the darkness, letting myself be as empty as the moonless sky. In that sacred void, something shifted. I realized gratitude has its own cycles, just like the moon.

The next few weeks became a profound experiment. Instead of forcing daily gratitude practices, I began following nature's rhythms. During the dark moon, I allowed myself quiet reflection and gentle acknowledgment. As the moon grew, so did my appreciation. By full moon, I found myself naturally celebrating life's abundance. And as the moon waned, I released what no longer served my gratitude practice.

This rhythm revealed itself in daily cycles too. One evening in my tiny apartment bathroom, exhausted from treatment, I discovered my natural gratitude peak arrived during my evening shower. The warm water, the quiet space, the end-of-day surrender - it created perfect conditions for genuine thankfulness. No forcing needed.

I started small - appreciating the miracle of hot water, the privacy of my own bathroom, the simple luxury of soap and clean towels. From this seed, natural rhythms of gratitude began emerging throughout my day. Dawn became a time for whispered thanks. Midday brought moments of sunlit appreciation. Dusk gathered the day's gifts. Night welcomed deeper recognition.

But here's what's fascinating - your rhythm might be completely different. During my teaching travels, I've met people whose gratitude flows strongest during morning coffee, others who find it during their commute, some who connect deeply during workouts. There's no "right" time for gratitude. There's only your time.

I witnessed the power of this understanding during my IRS journey. Instead of trying to feel grateful about my impossible debt (let's be honest - who feels naturally thankful for tax problems?), I followed the threads of genuine appreciation where they appeared. Sometimes it was as simple as acknowledging the sunrise during my morning walks, or recognizing the unexpected kindness of an IRS agent. Each authentic moment, offered in its own perfect timing, created space for more to flow.

This is the feminine way of gratitude - not a rigid practice to perfect, but a natural dance to embody. Sometimes we lead with conscious appreciation. Sometimes we follow life's gentle prompts. Sometimes we simply pause to feel the music of existence moving through us.

Your body already knows this dance. Your cells remember this rhythm. Your heart beats in this natural pattern of give and receive, expand and contract, appreciate and release. Trust this knowing. It will guide you to your own perfect gratitude flow.

I used to think creating sacred space meant having the perfect meditation room, complete with crystals, candles, and all the spiritual trappings. My tiny apartment during cancer treatment taught me something different. Sacred space begins in the body and radiates outward from there.

I discovered this truth one morning during radiation. Sitting in the sterile hospital waiting room, feeling anything but spiritual, I placed my hand on my heart - a simple gesture that would transform my understanding of sacred space. In that moment, my body became a sanctuary. No crystals needed, no special altar required. Just the warmth of my palm, the rhythm of my breath, and the quiet gathering of appreciation in my heart.

This portable sanctuary served me everywhere - during tense meetings with the IRS, in doctors' offices, even while paying seemingly impossible medical bills. But something even more beautiful emerged from this practice. Once I recognized my body as the first sacred space, creating external sanctuaries became natural and effortless.

My tiny apartment during recovery became a laboratory for this understanding. With barely enough room for a bed and basic furniture, I discovered that sacred space isn't about size - it's about intention. A single candle in the corner became my morning gratitude anchor. The windowsill, blessed with natural light, transformed into my midday pause point. My simple bed, draped with a soft blanket, offered evening sanctuary.

One of my clients, Isabelle, found her sacred space in her car during lunch breaks. "It's the only quiet place I have," she told me. Another transformed her daily shower into a gratitude temple with nothing more than intention and a few drops of lavender oil. The location doesn't matter - it's the sacredness we bring to it that creates the magic.

These days, my gratitude altar fits on one corner of my desk - a rose quartz crystal, a simple intention written on beautiful paper, a fresh flower when available. It's not elaborate, but it reminds me to pause, to appreciate, to open to receiving. Some mornings, I simply sit with my coffee near this small sacred space, letting appreciation flow naturally.

Your sanctuary might be a corner of your bedroom, a quiet spot in your garden, or your favorite chair. You might find it in the early morning kitchen as you prepare tea, or in the evening as you watch the sunset. The key isn't the location - it's the sacred intention you bring to it.

Think of these spaces as gratitude anchors in your day - not obligations to fulfill, but invitations to remember. They're like friends waiting to welcome you home to yourself, reminding you of the abundance that's always present.

These sacred spaces naturally give birth to sacred practices. I remember the first morning I sat in my tiny gratitude corner during cancer treatment. Instead of forcing myself through a rigid spiritual routine, I simply let the space hold me. That single candle, the comfortable cushion, the morning light - they invited their own kind of practice.

My natural rhythm emerged from this space. Some mornings called for quiet stillness, others for gentle movement. Sometimes I wrote in my journal, other times I just sat with my tea. The practice followed the space, which followed my body's wisdom.

Trust this wisdom. Your cells know the way to genuine gratitude. Let them guide your practice.

Daily Sacred Practices

Think of these practices like tending a garden - each small act of attention helps gratitude grow naturally and abundantly. I transformed rigid "gratitude requirements" into flowing sacred moments that actually stuck. Let me share what my morning rituals actually look like, how they evolved from desperate spiritual practices into natural rhythms of gratitude. It's quite different from what you might expect.

My mornings once started with panic - checking emails, worrying about bills, mentally calculating how to survive another day. During my cancer journey, that all changed, not because I forced it, but because I was too exhausted to maintain the anxiety.

I remember the exact morning this shift began. I was lying in bed, too tired from radiation to jump into my usual stress spiral. Instead of reaching for my phone, I just lay there, feeling the warmth of my blankets, listening to early birds outside my window. Something profound happened in that simple moment - I discovered what true morning sanctuary felt like.

These days, my morning unfolds like a gentle dance. Sometimes it starts before sunrise when I'm in my Caribbean home, other times it begins later in my Texas space. The time doesn't matter - it's the quality of presence that creates the magic.

Let me take you through an actual morning. I wake naturally, keeping my eyes closed for those first precious moments. Instead of planning my day or worrying about what's ahead, I simply feel my breath, notice the sheets against my skin, appreciate the gift of another dawn. Not as a spiritual practice, but as genuine recognition of what's already here.

My morning tea ritual evolved during treatment when I couldn't stomach coffee anymore. Now it's become a sacred pause I look forward to. I remember one particular morning when this ritual showed me its true power. I had just received another overwhelming medical bill, and my old pattern would have been to dive straight into panic with my first sip. Instead, I found myself fully present with just my tea - feeling its warmth, watching steam rise, appreciating this simple luxury. By the time I finished that cup, solutions for the bill had naturally emerged in my mind.

Midday presented its own challenges during my healing journey. I couldn't maintain long meditation sessions between treatments, so I discovered something more powerful - micro-moments of gratitude. Standing in line at the pharmacy, instead of stressing about how long the line was, I'd take three conscious breaths and find one thing to appreciate. Maybe it was the pharmacist's kind smile or the needed prescriptions which would soothe my pain, were filled. These tiny pauses began creating something remarkable - a continuous flow of gratitude that carried me through each day.

Evenings became especially precious. After days filled with medical appointments and business decisions, I needed a way to shift from doing to being. I started what I call my "gentle completion ritual." No lengthy spiritual practices - just simple moments of recognition. Maybe lighting a candle while reviewing the day's gifts, or taking an appreciative shower letting gratitude wash over me along with the water.

The beauty of these rituals is their flexibility. Some days they're elaborate, other days they're brief. During treatment, sometimes all I could manage was one conscious breath. That was enough. It's not about perfectly executing a spiritual practice - it's about finding your natural gratitude rhythm.

Special moments get their own recognition too. Full moons, changing seasons, even paying bills become opportunities for appreciation. I remember looking at a particularly large medical bill and instead of feeling dread, finding myself grateful for the treatment it represented. That's when I knew these practices had transformed from something I do into someone I am. Your own gratitude rhythm will be uniquely yours. Trust your body's wisdom about what feels natural. Some people love elaborate rituals; others find deeper meaning in simple pauses. There's no right way to recognize abundance - there's only your way.

I discovered this truth during my deepest healing moments. The practices that emerged weren't from books or teachers, but from my own body's wisdom. Every cell knows how to receive, how to appreciate, how to flow with life's natural abundance. My journey taught me to trust this inner knowing above any external system or structure.

Trust this wisdom. Your cells know the way to genuine gratitude.

Let them guide your practice.

Chapter 6

THE FLOW OF GIVING

Standing at the edge of the Pacific Ocean one morning during my cancer recovery, watching waves roll in and out with perfect rhythm, I had one of those "aha" moments that changes everything. There I was, worried about medical bills, no health insurance, and an empty bank account which seemed bigger than the Pacific - when nature handed me the answer I'd been seeking.

Every wave that rolled in had to roll out. The ocean wasn't trying to hold onto its water. It wasn't worried about running out. It simply trusted the eternal dance of giving and receiving. This is Spiritual Economics in its purest form.

I laughed out loud (probably causing nearby joggers to give me concerned looks). Here I was, clutching every dollar like it was my last, while the entire universe was demonstrating a different way of being. The ocean, the ultimate abundance teacher, was showing me what my spiritual mentors had been trying to tell me for years: true prosperity isn't about holding on - it's about staying in the flow.

Understanding Spiritual Economics

Let me be clear - spiritual economics isn't some woo-woo concept divorced from reality. It's as practical as gravity and just as consistent. Just like there are physical laws that govern our material world, there are spiritual laws that govern the flow of abundance. I had to learn these laws the hard way, through trial and error (mostly error), but you don't have to. I discovered this truth in the most unlikely place - sitting in my oncologist's office, reviewing the staggering costs of treatment, when something profound struck me. Just like the ocean before me, life was inviting me to participate in a greater flow. Every resource I needed was somehow appearing - kind nurses, financial advisors, unexpected support. Yet my instinct was to hold tight, to conserve, to contract in fear.

Spiritual economics operates on principles quite different from conventional financial wisdom. Eric Butterworth's work transformed my understanding completely. While traditional economics focuses on scarcity and competition, spiritual economics reveals a universe of infinite supply and eternal circulation. Let me share how I discovered these principles through both my darkest trials and greatest transformations. This wasn't about manifesting millions or visualizing wealth. It was about understanding fundamental spiritual laws that govern abundance.

It appears simple yet it is so profound. Like breathing, what flows out creates space for more to flow in. An exhale must precede an inhale. You must create a receiving capacity through the giving away of what you desire and it becomes a circle, (circulation) instead of stagnation. What will constrict this flow, this circulation is fear, what opens it up is trust. The tighter you hold onto money the more you block the flow of more of it into your life. Generosity and giving opens up this channel as trust activates it. In the previous chapters I shared about gratitude. What you appreciate expands, blessings multiply when you share them, the simple truth is "giving" amplifies worth and abundance.

When I began applying these principles during my cancer journey, something remarkable happened. Despite having less materially than ever before, I experienced a profound sense of wealth. Every time I found a way to give - even just a genuine thank you to my nurses - more support would mysteriously appear.

Spiritual economics operates on four fundamental principles that completely contradict conventional financial wisdom:

1. Giving increases receiving (I know - it sounds backwards, but stay with me)
2. Circulation creates expansion (like a muscle growing stronger through use)
3. Fear constricts, trust expands (your consciousness literally shapes your reality)
4. What we bless multiplies (even if it's leaving our lives)

Think about it. Does a fruit tree hoard its apples? Does the sun charge per ray? Does a rose demand payment for its fragrance? Nature understands what we humans often forget - giving isn't a loss, it's participation in the cosmic dance of abundance.

When I first encountered these principles during my darkest financial times, my immediate response was resistance. "Sure," I thought, "that's fine for trees and oceans - they don't have an IRS agent breathing down their neck." But here's what shifted everything for me: The universe doesn't respond to what we have or don't have. It responds to our consciousness about what we have.

Let me give you a practical example. After my Christmas eating cookies from the Dollar Store, I had exactly $12 to my name. My spiritual teacher suggested I start giving 10% of whatever came in. My first thought? "You don't understand - I have nothing to give!" But what I really meant was, "I'm too terrified to give. What if I need that money?"

That's when she shared something that would transform not just my finances, but my entire relationship with abundance: "Debbie," she said, "the universe doesn't check your bank balance before deciding whether to support you. It responds to your willingness to participate in the flow."

The first time I actually tested these principles, I started small - embarrassingly small. I began blessing my bills as I paid them (yes, even the big scary ones). I'd thank the electric company for keeping my lights on, the phone company for keeping me connected, even the credit card companies for their previous trust in me. Was I still scared? Absolutely. But something began shifting in my consciousness.

Here's what most prosperity teachers don't tell you: The amount doesn't matter nearly as much as the consciousness behind it. A dollar given in trust creates more abundance than a thousand dollars given in fear. I discovered this truth while paying those seemingly endless bills. When I shifted from "I have to pay" to "I get to circulate abundance," everything changed.

But let me be real with you - this isn't about magical thinking. Spiritual economics is as practical as a bank statement and as consistent as compound interest. The difference is, it operates on spiritual principles rather than just material mechanics.

Think of it like learning to swim. You can study water dynamics and buoyancy calculations all day long, but at some point, you have to get in the water. That's what spiritual economics asks of us - not just to understand the principles, but to live them.

Your Prosperity Pulse Check

Pull out your journal and try this on. First notice your immediate response to these statements:

> *"There is always more than enough"*
> *"Giving creates increase"*
> *"Money flows naturally to me"*
> *"I trust in infinite supply"*

Now rate (from 1-10 – 1 being never and 10 being always), your current relationship with:

Giving freely

Receiving gracefully

Trusting abundance

Blessing money as it flows out

This isn't about judging where you are - it's about honestly assessing your starting point for transformation. Remember: You can't redirect a river until you know which way it's currently flowing.

Learning to Give When I Had Nothing

Let me tell you about the moment I thought my spiritual teacher had completely lost her mind. There I was, sitting in her cozy office filled with crystals and angel cards, attempting to explain my impossible financial situation. I had a six-figure IRS debt that was growing faster than kudzu in summer, a mortgage business that felt like it was held together with duct tape and prayers, and a bank account that was running on fumes. I was doing that thing we all do when we're scared - talking fast, making excuses, building my case for why my situation was different, special, impossible.

That's when she did something that changed everything - she just sat there in complete silence, letting my words run out of steam. When I finally stopped talking, she looked me straight in the eyes and said something that seemed absolutely crazy: "Start giving ten percent of everything that comes in."

I actually laughed out loud. Not a joyful laugh, mind you, but that kind of desperate, are-you-f-ing-kidding-me laugh that comes when someone suggests something so far outside your reality that it seems absurd. "Did you not hear what I just said? I have over $350,000 in IRS debt. I'm barely keeping my lights on. I have NOTHING to give!"

She just smiled that knowing smile spiritual teachers seem to perfect and said, "That's exactly why you need to start giving."

Here's what she understood that I didn't: My "nothing to give" story wasn't about my bank balance - it was about my terror of letting go. I was operating like a spiritual hoarder, clutching every dollar so tightly, I was literally cutting off the flow of abundance. Like trying to hold onto a handful of sand, the tighter I gripped, the more slipped through my fingers.

The next few weeks were a masterclass in resistance. I had every excuse in the book:

- "I'll start giving when the IRS debt is handled"
- "I need to be responsible and pay my bills first"
- "I can't give money, but I give my time"
- "What if I give and then need that money?"

Each excuse sounded so logical, so responsible. But they were all just fear wearing a business suit called excuses.

Finally, in what felt like equal parts terror and defiance, I started giving. I started small - embarrassingly small. I'd put a single dollar in the collection basket at church, feeling like the widow with her mite. But here's what was different: Instead of giving from guilt or obligation, I began giving with real intention. That dollar wasn't just currency - it was my declaration of trust in the universe's abundance.

Let me be clear - this isn't one of those spiritual bypass stories where I started tithing and suddenly all my problems magically disappeared. What happened was both more subtle and more profound. As I developed a giving practice, even in tiny amounts, my relationship with money began to shift. The stranglehold of scarcity thinking started to loosen its grip.

I started noticing something fascinating: On the weeks I committed to giving first - even tiny amounts - money seemed to flow more easily. Unexpected clients would show up. Past due commissions would suddenly come through. It wasn't dramatic, but it was consistent enough to get my attention.

The real miracle wasn't in my bank account (at least not at first) - it was in my consciousness. Each small act of giving was like a declaration: "I trust there will be more." Even when everything logical screamed the opposite, I kept returning to that trust. I started with one percent of my income, then two, gradually working my way toward that seemingly impossible ten percent.

What I discovered through this process shocked me: Giving wasn't depleting my resources - it was actually creating space for more to flow in. It was like I'd been living in a stagnant pond, desperately trying to hold onto every drop, when what I really needed was to create movement, to participate in the flow.

The most profound shifts happened when I began blessing my bills as I paid them. Yes, even the IRS notices. Instead of sending payments wrapped in resentment and fear, I started thanking each creditor for what they'd provided. This wasn't just positive thinking - it was a fundamental shift in how I understood the circulation of money.

The real turning point came during a particularly rough month when two big loan closings fell through. I was sitting at my desk, staring at a pile of bills, when I remembered something my spiritual teacher had said: "The times you least want to give are the times you most need to."

Instead of panicking, I did something that seemed completely counterintuitive - I wrote a check to my church for $100. It wasn't much compared to what I used to make, but in that moment, it felt like handing over my last lifeline. My hands were literally shaking as I wrote it.

Here's the thing about giving when you're scared - it does something to your brain chemistry. You can't be in fear and trust at the same time. By choosing to give despite my fear, I was literally rewiring my neural pathways around money.

The next week, something bizarre happened. An old client called out of the blue about refinancing their house. Then another. Then another. Within three weeks, I had more business than I'd had in the previous three months. Was it coincidence? Maybe. But I'd been in the mortgage business long enough to know that this kind of synchronicity wasn't normal.

But here's what really blew my mind: The more I gave, the more I noticed abundance everywhere - not just in my bank account. I started seeing opportunities I'd been blind to before. Solutions to my IRS situation began appearing. People who could help showed up in unexpected ways.

It wasn't that the universe had suddenly become more generous. I had become more receptive. Every act of giving was like cleaning another window in my abundance awareness, letting in more light.

Remember that IRS debt that seemed bigger than Texas? As I continued my giving practice, something shifted in how I approached it. Instead of seeing it as a punishment or burden, I began seeing it as an opportunity to demonstrate trust. I even started blessing the IRS agents handling my case (though I'll admit, that took some practice).

The resolution, when it came, was nothing short of miraculous. But here's what I know now - the miracle wasn't in the external solution. The miracle was in my transformed relationship with abundance itself.

Through this journey, I learned something profound about spiritual economics: It's not about the money. It's never been about the money. It's about our willingness to participate in the flow of life itself.

When I finally understood this - really understood it in my bones - everything changed. Giving wasn't something I did anymore; it became who I was. Whether I was sharing knowledge, offering support, or writing checks, I had become a conduit for abundance rather than a container trying to hold it.

Creating your Giving Plan
Let me share something that still makes me laugh. There I was, fresh from my "get over yourself" moment in financial freedom class, trying to create the perfect giving plan. I had my spreadsheets ready, my calculator handy,

determined to mathematically figure out the exact right percentage to give. Talk about missing the point entirely!

The universe, with its infinite sense of humor, had other plans for teaching me about giving. It started in that radiation waiting room, where I found myself broke but somehow peaceful. A woman next to me was crying softly. Without thinking, I reached into my purse and offered her my last tissue. That simple gesture taught me more about giving than all my careful calculations ever had.

Taking Your Giving Temperature

Before I tell you how to create your own giving practice, let's do what I had to do - get brutally honest about where you are right now. I remember sitting in my tiny apartment after another radiation treatment, finally ready to face my true feelings about giving.

I grabbed my journal and wrote: "When I think about giving money, I feel terrified." Not very spiritual, but oh so true. My biggest fear? That I'd give away what I needed for survival. What stopped me from giving more? The endless loop in my head screaming, "But what about the medical bills?"

Let me tell you what happened next. Instead of trying to force myself into some holy-roller version of generosity, I started where I was. I rated my comfort with giving on a scale of 1-10. Giving money to others? A shaky 3. Receiving from others? An embarrassing 1 (hello, control issues!). Regular charitable giving? Maybe a 4 on a good day.

The Consciousness Shift

This is where it gets interesting. During one particularly sleepless night, wrestling with whether to make a small donation to my spiritual center, I had a revelation. The voice in my head that said "I would give more if..." was the same voice that said "I'll never get out of IRS debt." Same energy, different costume.

I started tracking patterns in my giving - or more accurately, my not- giving. When did I give freely? Usually in small, spontaneous moments, like buying coffee for the person behind me in line. When did I hesitate? Any time it involved planned giving or larger amounts. The pattern was clear - I trusted my heart's spontaneous generosity but not my mind's planned giving.

Creating Your Natural Giving Rhythm

Here's where most giving plans go wrong - they try to force natural generosity into unnatural structures. Instead of setting rigid rules, I began what I call "organic giving practice."

I started exactly where I was:

Current income? Barely covering medical bills.

Comfortable giving percentage? One percent (yes, really - I started that small).

Desired giving percentage? Ten percent (eventually, maybe, if the sky didn't fall).

But here's what transformed everything - instead of forcing myself to jump from 1% to 10%, I created what I call "giving stepping stones." Each small increase built confidence for the next. It's like learning to swim - you don't start in the deep end.

The Universal ATM

Speaking of swimming pools - here's a metaphor that changed everything for me. One day, after another sleepless night worrying about medical bills, I was standing at the hospital ATM. As I inserted my card (praying there were sufficient funds), something clicked. The universe works exactly like this ATM - you have to put something in before you can get something out.

But here's what most people miss, and what I certainly didn't understand during my mortgage business years: The ATM doesn't create money - it just facilitates flow. Similarly, when we give, we're not creating abundance - we're participating in its natural circulation.

Breaking Free from "Not Enough"

My own dance with "not enough" is quite a story. During my high-flying lending days, I could explain compound interest in my sleep. I could structure million-dollar loans over breakfast. Yet no matter how much money flowed through my hands, that whisper of "not enough" followed me like a shadow.

Then came the ultimate irony - facing cancer without health insurance. Talk about a crash course in "not enough"! But here's where it gets interesting. Lying in that hospital bed, technically at my poorest - no income, mounting medical bills, uncertain future - I finally understood something profound: The difference between actual scarcity (my bank balance) and scarcity consciousness (my inner state) is like the difference between being in a rainstorm and being afraid of water.

The Anatomy of "Not Enough"

Picture this: There I was, running a successful business, helping others create wealth, generating substantial income - the very picture of external success. Meanwhile, my internal reality looked more like a horror movie:

> *Every night, I'd wake up in stressed about money*
> *Every day, I'd feel unworthy of my success*
> *Every moment, anxiety gnawed at my peace*

I was like someone standing in the rain complaining of thirst. Abundance was literally pouring down around me, but my "not enough" consciousness was like an invisible umbrella of resistance.

Breaking Free Begins Within

The shift began in the most unexpected place - during a conversation with my radiologist. She was explaining how radiation worked, and suddenly everything about abundance became crystal clear. "Your body's receptivity to the treatment," she explained, "matters more than the amount of radiation we give you. Some patients can handle more, others less. It's not about the dose - it's about the capacity to receive."

I nearly fell off the exam table. Here was the perfect metaphor for my entire relationship with abundance. For years, I'd been focusing on the wrong thing - how to get more, make more, accumulate more. But just like radiation treatment, abundance was never about the quantity. It was about my capacity to receive.

This understanding began shifting everything. During my morning walks to treatment (because I couldn't afford hospital parking - oh, the ironies of life!), I started noticing how nature demonstrated this principle. Trees didn't strain to reach for sunlight - they grew naturally toward it. The morning dew didn't force itself to hydrate the grass - it simply allowed itself to be absorbed. Every living thing seemed to understand what I was just beginning to grasp: Receiving is as natural as breathing when we stop resisting it.

The Liberation Process
My liberation from "not enough" didn't happen in one dramatic moment. It was more like watching a sunrise - so gradual you barely notice the change until suddenly everything is illuminated. It began with simple awareness practices that grew from my daily hospital routine:

Waiting for treatment became my laboratory for observing scarcity thoughts. Instead of distracting myself with magazines or my phone, I'd notice when fear crept in. "Will I ever afford this?" would float through my mind, and instead of either believing it or fighting it, I'd just observe it, like watching clouds pass across the sky.

The hospital cafeteria became my training ground for what I call "The Interruption Technique." One day, staring at the prices, I caught myself in my usual "I can't afford this" thinking. But instead of letting that thought run its usual course, I interrupted it with a simple question: "Is that really true?" Not in a forcing-positive-thinking way, but with genuine curiosity.

Remember that tissue I mentioned earlier? It led to one of my most profound lessons in receptivity. The woman I gave it to insisted on buying me coffee the next day. My first instinct was to refuse - classic "not enough" behavior, believing I didn't deserve to receive. But something made me pause and simply say "thank you." That simple act of receiving opened a door I didn't even know was closed.

The Paradox of Enough

Here's what I discovered through countless client sessions and my own journey: "Enough" isn't a number - it's a state of consciousness. I've worked with billionaires who lived in constant fear of scarcity and people of modest means who experienced true abundance daily.

Let me share a story that perfectly illustrates this paradox. During my deepest financial struggles with the IRS, I met two clients in the same week. The first was worth over $10 million but couldn't sleep at night worrying about money. The second lived on a teacher's salary but radiated such peace around finances that people were naturally drawn to learn from her.

What was the difference? The billionaire was trying to achieve enough; the teacher was expressing enough. One was like a glass constantly trying to fill itself, the other like a fountain naturally overflowing.

From Understanding to Action

All these realizations - about the Universal ATM, breaking free from "not enough," understanding true receptivity - they're beautiful, but they mean nothing without practical application. Let me share how this understanding finally landed in real life and created the bridge to true abundance consciousness.

Remember that teacher I mentioned? She taught me something profound about giving that would change everything. "Start so small it almost seems silly," she said. "But start." So I did. I began with what I call my "pocket change practice" - literally giving away spare change. Yes, the woman who once structured million-dollar mortgages was starting with quarters and dimes. But here's what was different - it was genuine. No resistance, no fear, just natural flow.

From there, something remarkable began happening. Each small act of giving created space for more receiving. It wasn't magic - it was mathematics of a higher order. Like compound interest for the soul, each genuine gesture of generosity, no matter how tiny, multiplied itself in unexpected ways.

I remember the day I realized this transformation had taken root. I was reviewing my first post-cancer business opportunity, the first of what ended up being many house flipping adventures. In the past, I would have obsessed over the numbers, tried to negotiate every detail, worried about every expense. Instead, I found myself focusing on what I could give through this opportunity. The money? It worked itself out perfectly, almost as an afterthought.

The Bridge to Abundance Consciousness
This is where giving practice becomes something more - it becomes the gateway to activating your inner billionaire. Every genuine act of giving, every moment of true receiving, every conscious participation in circulation builds the foundation for what we'll explore next: aligning with abundance at the deepest level.

Think of it like learning to play music. First, you have to understand the basic principles - that's what we've covered with spiritual economics. Then you practice the scales - that's your giving practice. But eventually, you're ready to play full symphonies - that's what happens when you activate your Inner Bilionaire and align with abundance completely.

As we move into exploring this alignment, remember: Every small act of giving has prepared you for this next step. Every time you chose trust over fear, flow over resistance, giving over hoarding, you were building the foundation for what comes next.

Your Inner Billionaire

Your inner billionaire - that part of you that inherently understands and effortlessly creates abundance - isn't something you need to create. Like a radio signal that's always broadcasting, it's always present. Through your giving practice, you've been tuning the dial, improving the reception. Now it's time to turn up the volume and let that prosperity consciousness play at full strength.

Let's discover how to activate this natural abundance that's always been yours.

Chapter 7
ACTIVATING YOUR INNER BILLIONAIRE

The moon doesn't force its phases. The tide doesn't struggle to flow. A flower doesn't strain to bloom. When we align with universal law, prosperity becomes as natural as breathing. I learned this truth not through easy times, but through what seemed like my darkest moment - a cancer diagnosis that would ultimately reveal how powerfully these laws work, even when we can't see their purpose.

Just weeks after hearing "yep, it's rectal cancer" from my soon-to- retire doctor, I found myself sitting in my oncologist's office, reviewing treatment protocols that would cost more than I could imagine. No health insurance. No savings. No clear path forward. Yet something profound was happening - I was about to witness universal laws in action in a way that would transform not just my health, but my entire understanding of abundance.

I had been aware of these laws throughout my life but knowing about them and understanding them from a "knowingness perspective" are entirely different things. What are the Universal Laws of Prosperity and how did I come to know them intimately?

The Universal Laws of Prosperity

When you're sitting in a bathroom at 3 AM with a crack pipe in your hand, or staring at an IRS notice for $350,000, or hearing "yep, it's rectal cancer" from a doctor who clearly missed the bedside manner class in medical school, the last thing you're thinking about is universal laws. Trust me, I've been there - all three places, actually.

But here's the thing that blew my mind when I finally got it: These laws were working the whole time, even when I was absolutely certain the universe had put me in cosmic time-out. They're like gravity - whether you believe in them or not, they're still doing their thing. And once you understand them? Holy moly, does life get interesting.

Law of Divine Timing

Remember that scene in The Wizard of Oz where everything lines up perfectly - the tornado, the house landing, the ruby slippers? That's divine timing. Except in real life, it usually doesn't look so perfect in the moment.

Take my cancer diagnosis. No health insurance, barely making ends meet - terrible timing, right? Wrong. It happened exactly when California's Medicaid system could fully support me. Had it been a year earlier or later, I might've been writing this book from a cardboard box under a bridge.

Even my addiction - and trust me, for years I thought that was just the universe's way of saying "Gotcha!" - happened in divine timing. Without that experience, I wouldn't be able to help others transform their lives now. Though I have to admit, there probably were easier ways to develop empathy than smoking crack, but hey, I've never been one for taking the easy road.

The Law of Circulation

During my mortgage broker days, I was the queen of manifesting money - and then watching it vanish faster than a pizza at a Weight Watchers meeting. I could close six-figure deals Monday morning and be broke by Friday afternoon.

That wasn't just poor money management (though let's be honest, my financial planning back then consisted of knowing which ATMs were open at 2 AM). It was the Law of Circulation trying to teach me something.

Money, like energy, has to flow. Think of it like blood circulation - if it stops moving, that's not a good thing. I learned this lesson the hard way, but then again, that's kind of my specialty. Even when I was living on food stamps during cancer treatment, I discovered you can always participate in circulation. Sometimes it's just through a smile, a kind word, or letting someone ahead of you in line at the grocery store (though maybe not when you're holding the last package of Oreos).

Law of Correspondence

"As within, so without" - sounds like something you'd find on a yoga studio wall next to a picture of a sunset, right? But here's the real deal: During my Texas years, I was like a money magician - could manifest large sums through my mortgage business faster than you could say "balloon payment." But keeping it? That was like trying to hold onto a greased pig at a county fair.

Why? Because my inner state matched my outer reality perfectly - like one of those "Who Wore It Better?" fashion face-offs, except both contestants were my own self-sabotage. I didn't believe I deserved lasting prosperity, so I created situations that proved me right. Talk about a self-fulfilling prophecy - I was writing bestsellers in the art of proving myself unworthy.

Law of Attraction

Ah, the celebrity of universal laws - thanks to that little book that had everyone putting Ferraris on their vision boards. But here's what they don't tell you in the movie: It's not about attracting what you want; it's about being what you are.

During my healing journey, I stopped trying to "attract" health and wealth like I was some kind of cosmic magnet. Instead, I started being well, despite what my body and bank account were saying. I taught prosperity principles from my hospital bed (talk about walking your talk - or in my case, lying down your talk). The universe doesn't respond to your Wishlist - it responds to your frequency. And let me tell you, finding your prosperity frequency while wearing a hospital gown that opens in the back? That's some advanced manifestation work right there.

Everything Is Working Together

Here's the mind-bender - these laws aren't like separate menu items at a cosmic cafeteria where you can pick and choose. They're more like ingredients in your grandmother's secret recipe - leave one out and the whole thing falls flat.

I watched this play out during my move from California to Texas. Divine Timing lined up the perfect moment (even though my logical mind was screaming "ARE YOU CRAZY?"). Correspondence made sure my inner readiness matched the outer opportunity. Non-Resistance helped me flow through the changes instead of fighting them (though I still had my moments of wanting to drag my heels like a toddler at bedtime).

The moon doesn't force its phases. The tide doesn't struggle to flow. A flower doesn't strain to bloom. And you, my friend, don't need to force your prosperity. You just need to understand the laws that are already working in your favor - even when it looks like they're working against you.

Now, as I split my time between Texas and the Caribbean (still pinching myself about that one), teaching these principles internationally, I can see how every experience - from the crack pipe to the cancer ward to the corner office - was orchestrated by these perfect laws. Your journey might look different from mine (and for your sake, I hope it involves fewer trips to rehab), but these same laws are working in your life right now.

The question isn't whether they're working - it's whether you're ready to dance with them instead of wrestling them to the ground. Trust me, the dance is way more fun.

How Synchronicity Began Appearing

Remember that moment in Raiders of the Lost Ark when all the pieces line up perfectly for Indiana Jones to find the treasure? That's synchronicity - except in real life, it usually starts with you flat on your back in a hospital bed wondering if the universe has lost your address.

At least that's how it started for me. There I was, post-diagnosis, trying to figure out how to pay for treatments that cost more than my first house (which, given my history with the IRS, wasn't saying much). Then this woman in crisp white scrubs appears at my door like some kind of bureaucratic angel and asks, "Are you poor enough to qualify for California's Medicaid program?"

Now, if you'd told me this was synchronicity in action, I might have thrown my jello cup at you. But looking back? That "random" encounter kicked off a series of events that would make even Carl Jung raise an eyebrow.

When Coincidences Aren't Coincidental
Let me take you back to my mortgage broker days in Texas. I had this habit of "accidentally" meeting exactly the right client at exactly the right time - usually while buying chocolate chips at 2 AM (some habits die hard). At first, I chalked it up to luck. But then I started noticing a pattern. The more I aligned with these universal laws we just talked about, the more these "coincidences" started piling up like dirty dishes in a bachelor's sink. Except these weren't really coincidences - they were synchronicities, the universe's way of winking at you while simultaneously helping you level up.

The Magic Begins (No Wands Required)
It really kicked into high gear during my recovery journey. Picture this: I'm fresh out of rehab (again), trying to rebuild my life, when I get this inexplicable urge to visit a specific coffee shop - not my usual spot where they knew my chocolate chip muffin order by heart. There, I "randomly" meet someone who becomes crucial to my international teaching career.

Was it just caffeine-driven chance? About as much as my grandmother's secret sauce recipe was "just ketchup." These synchronicities were like cosmic text messages saying, "You're on the right track, kiddo" (yes, in my head, the universe talks like a 1940s movie star).

The Texas Two-Step of Synchronicity
My move to Texas? That whole adventure started with what I call "divine insomnia" - lying in my nephew's bunk bed during a visit, hearing this persistent inner voice saying "Move to Texas" like a spiritual GPS that wouldn't shut up. My logical mind had a field day with that one: "No job, no car, no place to live - and oh yeah, what about Grammie's 500-pound piano?"

But here's where synchronicity does its little dance: Within days of surrendering to that guidance, I was packed in a Ryder truck, had a $500 jalopy waiting for me, and landed a job in what was supposedly a dead market. Even the piano situation worked itself out (though that's another story involving two movers, a six-pack of cerveza, and what I'm pretty sure was divine intervention).

The Rhythm of Reality
The real beauty of synchronicity is that it builds momentum. Like a cosmic snowball rolling downhill, each aligned action attracts more synchronistic events. Before you know it, you're living a life that would have seemed impossible a few years earlier.

Take my current situation - splitting time between Texas and the Caribbean, teaching prosperity principles internationally. If you'd told me this was my future while I was sitting in that hospital room, I would have assumed you were sampling my pain medication.

The Formula (That Isn't Really a Formula)
Here's the thing about synchronicity - you can't force it like a toddler into winter boots. But you can create conditions where it flourishes. Stay open to

the ridiculous. When that inner voice says "Move to Texas" or "Call this random tax attorney," don't immediately shut it down with logic.

Follow the breadcrumbs. Those little nudges and coincidences? They're like cosmic post-it notes. Trust the timing. Sometimes what looks like terrible timing (hello, cancer with no insurance) turns out to be perfect orchestration.

Keep your sense of humor. The universe loves a good laugh, and sometimes its synchronicities come wrapped in packages that make you go "Really? This is how we're doing this?"

The Bottom Line

Synchronicity isn't just some woo-woo concept for people who have too many crystals (though I do have a pretty impressive collection). It's the natural result of aligning with universal laws. It's what happens when you stop wrestling life to the ground and start dancing with it instead.

And yes, sometimes that dance looks less like Fred Astaire and more like your uncle at a wedding reception after too many margaritas. But that's okay - synchronicity doesn't require perfection. It just requires willingness.

Trust me, if a former crack addict with a six-figure IRS debt and a cancer diagnosis can end up living her dreams between Texas and the Caribbean, teaching others how to create their own magic, you can create miracles. Synchronicity isn't just real - it's your birthright.

Ready to learn how to tap into this flow? Well, buckle up buttercup, because we're about to dive into some practices that'll make synchronicity your new normal.

Meditation and Visualization Practices

You know how everyone tells you meditation is just sitting quietly and clearing your mind? Yeah, that worked about as well for me as trying to herd cats.

Especially during my early recovery days when my mind had more bounce than a sugar-rushed toddler on a trampoline.

The Reality of Meditation (When Your Mind Won't Shut Up)

Let me tell you about my first attempt at meditation during rehab. There I was, trying to "empty my mind" while simultaneously planning my grocery list, reliving every embarrassing moment since third grade, and wondering if I'd remembered to feed my dog. Spoiler alert: I didn't even have a dog.

But here's what I discovered during those long minutes on the radiation table - meditation isn't about achieving some perfect state of mental silence. It's about finding your center in the middle of the chaos. Trust me, if I could find inner peace while a giant machine was buzzing around my nether regions, you can do this.

The Lazy Person's Guide to Meditation

Instead of forcing yourself into lotus position for an hour (who has that kind of hip flexibility anyway?), try what I call the "Coffee Cup Contemplation." It's simple here's how:

Take your morning coffee (or tea, or green juice if you're fancy), find a quiet spot, and just be present with your beverage. No phone, no TV, no solving the world's problems. Just you and your cup, having a moment.

I developed this practice during my mortgage days when I was too stressed to sit still. It became my sanctuary between closing deals and juggling client demands. Plus, it's socially acceptable - nobody questions you staring into your coffee cup. Try that with traditional meditation and people think you're plotting world domination.

Visualization: Beyond Vision Boards

I love a good vision board as much as the next personal development junkie. But after plastering my walls with pictures of beach houses and luxury cars during my broke years, I realized something: visualization isn't about creating a cosmic shopping list.

Remember my Caribbean dream? Instead of just picturing the beach house, I started feeling the freedom it represented. During my cancer treatments, I wouldn't just visualize health - I'd embody wellness, even while rocking that stylish hospital gown.

The Embodied Visualization Practice
This is where it gets juicy. Instead of just seeing what you want, you become it. Here's how:

Start with something simple - making tea works beautifully (sensing a theme here?). Feel your body's natural wisdom. Notice your hands as they work, your breath as it flows, your senses as they engage. This isn't about forcing visions - it's about allowing awareness.

I used this practice during my entire healing journey, and later during my transition to Texas. Instead of visualizing specific outcomes, I'd feel into my body's knowing. The results were remarkable - opportunities appeared that I couldn't have imagined to visualize.

The "Living It Now" Technique
One morning during my radiation treatments, while making tea (yes, again with the tea), a memory surfaced - watching my grandmother serve tea in her cherished china cups. She treated each cup like it held liquid gold, even though she bought her tea bags at the dollar store. That's when I got it: prosperity consciousness isn't about what you have, it's about how you experience what you have.

Try this: Take something ordinary in your life and treat it like it's extraordinary. Your morning shower? It's a luxury spa treatment. Your bed? It's a five-star hotel suite. Your workspace? It's a corner office with a view (even if it's actually your kitchen table with a view of your neighbor's garbage cans).

The Real Magic

Here's what transformed everything: When I stopped trying to use these practices to get somewhere else and started using them to fully inhabit where I was. Even during my darkest times - whether dealing with addiction, debt, or disease - I could find moments of pure presence.

Sure, sometimes my meditation looks more like controlled chaos than zen mastery. Sometimes my visualizations get interrupted by my to- do list. But that's okay - because the real magic isn't in doing it perfectly. It's in doing it consistently, with humor, grace, and the understanding that even imperfect practice is still practice.

Remember: You don't have to be a meditation master or visualization virtuoso to tap into your Inner Billionaire. You just need to be willing to show up, pay attention, and occasionally laugh at yourself while doing it.

Now, who's ready for another cup of tea?

Creating a Prosperity Consciousness

You know what's harder than getting out of debt? Getting out of a poverty mindset. Trust me, I managed to manifest large sums of money even while smoking crack, but keeping it? That required a complete consciousness overhaul.

The Poverty Hangover

Even after I'd cleaned up my act and started making good money again, I still found myself hoarding ketchup packets and calculating how many meals I could make from a box of pasta - behaviors left over from my "dollar store Christmas cookies" days. My bank account had changed, but my consciousness was still operating like I was one bad decision away from broke.

The Great Awakening (Not the Religious Kind)

The shift happened in the most unexpected place - during my cancer treatments. There I was, technically at my lowest point financially (unless you count that Christmas I spent alone with those dollar store cookies), when something clicked.

A nurse brought me an extra blanket without me asking, and instead of thinking "I need to save this for later" (yes, I had actually tried to smuggle hospital blankets before), I just received it with gratitude. Sounds small, right? But it was revolutionary for my prosperity consciousness.

The Receiving Lessons

Here's what I discovered: Most of us are terrible at receiving. We're like broken vending machines - money goes in, but nothing comes out. Or in my case, money went in and immediately found its way to the nearest crack dealer, on line buying site or taking others out to dinner. But that's not prosperity consciousness - that's just high-speed poverty.

> *I started practicing receiving in small ways:*
> *Accepting compliments without deflecting*
> *Taking help without feeling guilty*
> *Letting others pick up the check (this one was particularly challenging for*
> *my independent Texas spirit)*

The Money Conversations

You want to know where your prosperity consciousness needs work? Listen to how you talk about money. I used to say things like "I can't afford it" or "That's too expensive" faster than a Pentecostal preacher can say "Amen."

During my mortgage broker days, I could help clients see possibilities for their financial future while being completely blind to my own. Classic case of "teacher, teach thyself."

The Prosperity Practices

Here's what actually worked for me (and no, it doesn't involve burning sage or chanting affirmations at midnight):

1. The "Act As If" Game

Remember my first-class flight story? Instead of feeling out of place, I settled in like I belonged there. Because guess what? I did. We all do. Prosperity is our natural state - we just forget sometimes.

2. The Gratitude Flip

Every time I caught myself in scarcity thinking (like when I was calculating the price-per-square of toilet paper), I'd flip it to gratitude. "I have to pay these bills" became "I get to pay these bills because I have electricity/water/a roof over my head."

3. The Abundance Evidence Journal

Started keeping track of all the ways abundance showed up - from finding a parking spot right in front (if you've ever parked in downtown Los Angeles, you know that's a miracle) to manifesting Caribbean living.

The Reality Check

Look, creating a prosperity consciousness doesn't mean you'll never worry about money again. I still have moments when my old scarcity thinking tries to creep back in like an ex at 2 AM. The difference is, now I recognize it for what it is - just an old pattern, not my truth.

The Bottom Line

Your prosperity consciousness isn't something you create - it's something you uncover. Like cleaning years of gunk off a beautiful old mirror. The reflection was always clear underneath; you just couldn't see it.

And yes, sometimes the cleaning process involves some ugly crying in the bathroom (been there), or laughing at yourself when you realize you're still saving rubber bands "just in case" even though you're doing well financially (also been there).

The point isn't to become some enlightened money master who never has a negative thought about finances. It's about creating a new normal where prosperity feels as natural as breathing. Even if sometimes that breath catches a little when you look at your credit card bill.

Remember: If a former crack addict with a six-figure IRS debt can develop a prosperity consciousness strong enough to manifest international teaching and Caribbean living, you can too. It just takes practice, patience, and occasionally laughing at your own scarcity stories. Now, who's ready to start uncovering their natural state of abundance? (And no, that doesn't mean I'm picking up the check - we're working on prosperity consciousness here, not miracles.)

The Daily Abundance Alignment Practice

Here's a simple but powerful practice that transformed my life from crack houses to Caribbean beaches. No complicated rituals, no moon phases to track - just consistent alignment with abundance.

The Sacred Five Minutes

Every morning, before your feet hit the floor (or before you check your phone - I see you), take five sacred minutes:

1. Place one hand on your heart, one on your belly
2. Take three deep breaths
3. Feel one thing you're genuinely grateful for right now
4. Let your body remember what prosperity feels like
5. Ask: "What if everything is working in my favor today?"

That's it. Simple enough that you'll actually do it, powerful enough to shift your entire day.

The Prosperity Pause

Throughout your day, take brief "prosperity pauses" during these natural moments:

- Making your morning beverage
- Stopping at red lights
- Standing in line
- Paying bills
- Before starting work

During each pause, simply notice where abundance already exists. Maybe it's the ability to pay that bill, the coffee in your cup, or even just the breath in your body.

The Evening Integration

Before sleep, ask yourself three questions:

1. "Where did I notice abundance today?"
2. "What synchronicities appeared?"
3. "How am I different from who I was 24 hours ago?"

No journaling required (unless you want to). Just a moment of recognition before sleep.

Remember: This isn't about doing it perfectly. Some days you'll forget. Some days it'll feel mechanical. Some days you'll wonder if it's working at all. Keep going anyway.

I started this practice in a hospital bed during cancer treatment. If I could find abundance there, you can find it anywhere.

The universe is always speaking in the language of abundance. This practice simply helps you learn to listen.

Chapter 8
THE LANGUAGE OF WEALTH

If words were credit cards, I maxed out my scarcity vocabulary years ago. "I can't afford it." "Money doesn't grow on trees." "I'm broke." These phrases rolled off my tongue faster than chocolate chips disappearing from my mother's baking cupboard. And just like those childhood snack raids, my casual relationship with negative money talk had consequences I couldn't see coming.

How Words Shape Your Financial Reality

Let's travel back in time to the early 80's to my Pasadena office with spectacular view of the San Gabriel mountains - the office I helped pick out, right down to that massive oak desk that made me feel like a real somebody. I was the queen of the office, working for my then love interest who was both an attorney and blood stock agent. Money flowed through my hands like water through a sieve, which, as it turns out, was exactly the problem. This was long before I ever understood what abundance or prosperity was.

My life was magical in that moment. It's a typical Friday afternoon. I've just helped settle a massive case with my partner - the kind that should have set me up for months. I'm sitting at that impressive desk, staring at a proceeds check that was more than my parents made in a year. Instead of feeling successful, I immediately started planning ways to spend it, as if having it in my account was somehow dangerous. Same day, I helped a horse trainer whose income was a fraction of mine purchase a new race horse. I could see abundance was possible for them, but somehow, I remained convinced it wasn't possible for me, even though I had no concept of that at the time.

My unconscious thought pattern was: "You won't believe how quickly this money will disappear" while depositing the check. And wouldn't you know it? The universe, being the efficient delivery service it is, would make sure that money vanished faster than my sobriety at an open bar wedding. By Monday morning, I'd be back to counting quarters for gas money, wondering what cosmic joke I was the punchline of.

This pattern followed me everywhere, even into my drug days. I could manifest money like a magician pulling rabbits from a hat. Need quick cash for a fix? Watch me work my money magic. But keeping it? That was like trying to hold onto smoke. My words were programming me for a cycle of feast and famine faster than you could say "where's my dealer's number?"

Here's what took me decades to understand: Every word you speak about money is literally rewiring your brain. This isn't some metaphysical theory - though I've got enough crystals now to open a New Age shop. Neuroscience shows that each time you say "I can't afford it" or "Money is tight," you're actually building neural pathways of limitation. (See Chapter 4 for the science).

Think of your words as instructions to your nervous system. When you say "I'm broke," your body responds by constricting energy, tightening muscles, and shutting down your receiving channels. It's like putting up a "Closed for Business" sign in the universal abundance store.

During my Texas years, this truth became painfully clear. I remember sitting in my little rental office - a far cry from my Pasadena palace - looking at my bank balance after another successful closing. Instead of celebrating, I heard myself say, "Better enjoy it while it lasts." Guess what? It didn't last. Not because of any external circumstance, but because I had literally programmed my reality for temporary abundance.

The pivot point came during my cancer journey, of all places. There I was, in my oh-so-flattering hospital gown (whoever designed those clearly had a grudge against dignity), discussing treatment options with my oncologist. The cost numbers she was throwing around made my mortgage deals look like pocket change. My habitual "I can't afford this" was halfway out of my mouth when something shifted.

Maybe it was the drugs (the legal ones this time), maybe it was divine intervention, or maybe I was just finally tired enough of my own story, but I caught myself. Instead of completing that sentence, I heard myself ask, "What creative solutions are available?" The shift was subtle, but the impact was seismic.

That moment in the hospital with the blanket? It wasn't just about gratitude. It was my first real glimpse into how profoundly our words shape our reality. Like that time in Texas when I was teaching a prosperity workshop (oh, the irony - me, fresh out of treatment, teaching others about abundance). I heard myself telling participants, "Money flows to those who are open to receiving it," and suddenly realized I'd been about as open to receiving as a bank vault on Sunday.

Think about it - during my mortgage days, I could manifest six-figure deals out of thin air, yet somehow managed to stay broker than a three-legged card table. Why? Because every time money showed up, I'd unconsciously sabotage it with my words: "This won't last." "Better spend it before it disappears." "I don't deserve this." The universe, being the diligent customer service rep it is, made sure to fulfill every one of those orders with frightening efficiency.

Let me share something that happened during my first year of international teaching. I was in New York, about to lead a workshop on financial freedom (again with the irony - the universe has a wicked sense of humor). Just before going on stage, I caught myself saying, "Who am I to teach this? I used to smoke my mortgage payments." That's when it hit me - my words weren't just expressing doubt, they were creating it. Every self-deprecating comment was like writing a cosmic prescription for imposter syndrome.

Here's the wild part: Even during my addiction years, I was a master manifestor. Need money for drugs? Watch me pull a closing out of thin air. Need to convince a client to trust me despite being higher than a weather balloon? No problem. My words had power - I was just using them to create chaos instead of clarity.

During my cancer treatment, I noticed something fascinating. The patients who spoke about their healing as a certainty - even while hooked up to chemo - seemed to have better outcomes than those who constantly voiced doubt. Was it just positive thinking? Not exactly. Their words were literally programming their bodies for healing, just as my financial words had been programming my life for scarcity.

Remember my $350,000 IRS debt? The shift started the day I changed "I'll never get out of this" to "I'm finding creative solutions." Suddenly, opportunities started appearing. A tax advocate who specialized in impossible cases. An unexpected inheritance. A business opportunity that perfectly aligned with my skills. Was it magic? No - it was simply my words finally aligning with possibilities instead of problems.

But here's what really cooked my noodle: The same mouth that had been declaring poverty was also capable of speaking abundance into existence. The same tongue that had ordered up scarcity could just as easily place an order for prosperity. It wasn't about learning new words - it was about understanding the power of the ones I was already using.

Take my move to Texas. When I first heard that inner voice saying "Move to Texas," my words were all about why it was impossible. No job, no car, no place to live - oh, and let's not forget Grammie's 500-pound piano. But the moment I shifted from "I can't because..." to "I wonder how..." everything changed.

Within days, I had a Ryder truck, a $500 jalopy waiting for me, and a job in what was supposedly a dead market.

Words aren't just descriptive - they're prescriptive. Each phrase you utter is like placing an order with the cosmic kitchen. "I'm broke" is basically asking the universe for another serving of brokeness. "I can't afford it" is like signing up for the Scarcity of the Month Club.

When I finally understood that my words were painting my financial reality, I started listening to myself like a hawk watching its prey. And boy, what I heard wasn't pretty. My daily conversations were like a masterclass in poverty consciousness:

- In business meetings: "My rates are probably too high, but..."
- At the grocery store: "I should stick to the generic brands."
- With friends: "Must be nice to afford organic."

Each phrase was like a little poison dart aimed straight at my prosperity. But here's the thing about awareness - once you see it, you can't unsee it. Like that time during my cancer treatment when I caught myself saying, "I hope I can afford this" to my oncologist. Mid-sentence, I stopped and rephrased: "I trust that resources will appear for my healing." The nurse dropped her clipboard. Turns out she was on the committee that helped patients find financial assistance. Coincidence? About as much as finding a parking spot in downtown LA during rush hour.

The transformation wasn't overnight. At first, trying to speak prosperity felt about as natural as wearing a ball gown to a crack house. I remember standing in line at Whole Foods (back when it was still called "Whole Paycheck"), starting to say "I can't afford this" and catching myself. Instead, I said out loud, "I'm choosing to invest in my health." The woman behind me smiled and said, "That's exactly how I think about it." We ended up talking about her investment business, which led to a client referral worth ten times my grocery bill.

But let's be real - changing your vocabulary isn't just about swapping "can't afford" for "choosing to invest." During my international teaching phase, I had to completely rewire how I talked about money. Gone were the self-deprecating jokes about being a "reformed financial disaster." Instead, I started owning my journey: "I've learned powerful lessons about prosperity that I now share with others."

The shift really hit home during a workshop in Australia. A participant asked about my IRS debt story, expecting the usual "broke to woke" narrative. Instead of my rehearsed "I was a financial mess" speech, I heard myself say, "I was a master manifestor who needed to redirect my manifesting powers." The entire room's energy changed. Why? Because my words had finally aligned with my truth.

Remember that 500-pound piano that almost kept me from moving to Texas? My old vocabulary would have made it an insurmountable obstacle. My new vocabulary turned it into a perfect metaphor for transformation. "If I can move this piano," I started telling myself, "I can move any obstacle in my life." Spoiler alert: The piano situation resolved itself so smoothly it was almost comical.

Creating Real Affirmations That Actually Work

Most affirmations have about as much power as a motivational poster in a dentist's office. You know the kind I mean - standing in front of your mirror chanting "I am wealthy" while your bank account is laughing hysterically. I tried that approach during my IRS days. Spoiler alert: The IRS wasn't impressed by my positive thinking.

Here's the problem: Traditional affirmations are like trying to convince yourself you're on a beach in Hawaii while standing in a snowstorm in Minnesota. Your brain isn't stupid. It knows you're freezing, and no amount of "I am warm and tropical" is going to change that.

What I discovered through my own trial and error (heavy on the error) was that affirmations that actually work are like building a bridge from where you are to where you want to be. During my IRS journey, rather than saying "I am debt-free" (cue internal eye roll), I began using "I am finding creative solutions for financial freedom." This worked because it was true - I was finding solutions. It engaged my problem-solving brain instead of activating my inner skeptic.

Science backs this up (yeah, we're going there again). When you make statements your brain can believe, it starts creating new neural pathways instead of fighting you like a toddler at bedtime. Your nervous system relaxes instead of going into "liar, liar, pants on fire" mode.

Let me share what transformed my own affirmation practice. Remember that hospital room with the view of the San Gabriel mountains? Instead of trying to convince myself "I am perfectly healthy" (while literally hooked up to a morphine drip), I started affirming "I am supporting my body's natural healing wisdom." See the difference? One's a fantasy; the other's a pathway.

What about money? Instead of "I am a billionaire" (when my bank account was giving me side-eye), I used "I am learning to create and sustain wealth." This wasn't just positive thinking - it was creating a new reality one believable statement at a time.

Speaking Abundance into Existence
Want to know something wild? The universe takes your words as seriously as my old drug dealer took cash - no refunds, no exchanges, exact change only. Every word you speak is like placing an order with the cosmic kitchen, and honey, that kitchen never closes.

During my mortgage days, I would tell clients all day long how abundance was possible for them, while simultaneously telling myself I'd always struggle. Guess which statement the universe fulfilled? Here's a hint: It wasn't the abundant one.

Here's another juicy example. When I first dreamed of teaching internationally, my go-to phrase was "Who would want to learn from a former crack addict?" (Ever notice how we use our past as a weapon against our future?) Then I shifted to "My journey gives me unique insight into transformation." Within months, I was booking workshops in Australia and New Zealand. The universe doesn't care about your past - it cares about your present words.

But let's get really practical. I started playing what I call the "Prosperity Phrase Flip Game" in everyday situations:

At the grocery store:
    Old script: "I should stick to the generic brands."
    New script: "I'm making conscious choices about my resources."

Paying bills:
    Old script: "There goes all my money."
    New script: "I'm grateful for the services these payments provide."

In business:
    Old script: "My rates might be too high."
    New script: "I charge what my expertise is worth."

Here's the kicker - this isn't just word play. Every time you flip a scarcity statement to an abundance declaration, you're literally rewiring your brain's prosperity pathways. It's like updating your internal operating system from Scarcity 1.0 to Abundance 365.

Remember my $500 jalopy in Texas? Instead of saying "It's all I can afford," I started saying "This car is getting me to my next level." Within months, I manifested enough clients to upgrade. The car didn't change - my language about it did. Within months I had a newer car, then another newer car and finally paying cash for a brand new car off the show room floor.

During my international teaching phase, I noticed something fascinating. The participants who got the best results weren't the ones with the biggest vision boards or the fanciest affirmations. They were the ones who changed their daily prosperity vocabulary. One woman stopped saying "I'm drowning in debt" and started saying "I'm navigating my financial freedom." Within six months, she'd created a debt elimination plan that actually worked.

Think of your words as seeds. Every time you speak, you're planting something in your prosperity garden. "I can't afford it" plants weeds. "I'm choosing to invest elsewhere" plants possibilities. What are you growing with your daily vocabulary?

Creating Your Prosperity Declarations

How to be sure the Universe Takes Your Order
When I was in my late 20's I remember working at a bar called the Boar's Head. Every order had to be crystal clear - no one wants to end up with a Long Island Iced Tea when they ordered a lemonade. The universe works the same way, except instead of drink orders, it's taking dictation of your prosperity declarations.

Let me give you a practical exercise that transformed my own prosperity vocabulary. I call it "The Prosperity Phrase Flip Challenge" (catchy, right?).

First, grab yourself a small notebook - nothing fancy, though if you want to bedazzle it with abundance crystals, I won't judge. For one week, carry this notebook everywhere (yes, even to the bathroom – some of our best scarcity thoughts happen there).

Every time you catch yourself using a scarcity phrase, write it down. Don't judge it, don't try to fix it, just catch it like you're collecting evidence. Trust me, after years of explaining things to the IRS, I know about collecting evidence.

At the end of each day, sit down with your scarcity collection (and maybe a glass of wine - this can be eye-opening stuff). Now comes the fun part: Let's flip each phrase to its prosperity version.

Here are some real examples from my own journey:

The Money Flip:
- "I'm always broke" becomes "I'm learning to create sustainable wealth"
- "I'll never get out of debt" becomes "I'm discovering creative paths to financial freedom"
- "Why do bad things always happen to me?" becomes "What's the opportunity in this situation?"

The Worth Flip:
- "I don't deserve success" becomes "I'm worthy of all good things"
- "Who am I to charge that much?" becomes "My expertise has valuable impact"
- "I should be grateful for any job" becomes "I attract opportunities that honor my worth"

The Future Flip:
- "I'll probably fail" becomes "I'm gathering data for success"
- "This never works for me" becomes "I'm open to new possibilities"
- "I can't afford that" becomes "I'm choosing to direct my resources elsewhere"

But here's the secret sauce - these new declarations have to feel true for you. During my cancer journey, I couldn't honestly say "I am perfectly healthy," but I could say "I trust my body's wisdom" or "I welcome healing." See the difference?

Remember: This isn't about lying to yourself. It's about choosing words that open doors instead of slamming them shut. You're not denying reality; you're giving yourself permission to create a new one.

Here is a daily practice if you choose to incorporate it:

Morning Declaration:
Start each day by speaking one prosperity truth. Not some pie-in- the-sky affirmation, but something you can genuinely believe. Mine started with "I'm open to receiving today" when that was all I could honestly say.

Midday Catch and Flip:
Use your notebook to track scarcity statements. Flip them immediately. Yes, right there in the grocery store when you catch yourself saying "I can't afford organic." Flip it to "I'm making conscious choices about my nutrition."

Evening Integration:
Review your flips. Celebrate the ones that felt authentic. Adjust the ones that need tweaking. Remember, this is a practice, not a performance.

Think of it like learning a new language - the language of prosperity. At first, you'll feel like a tourist stumbling over unfamiliar phrases. Keep practicing. Soon you'll be dreaming in abundance.

And here's the best part - unlike my old drug dealer, the universe has an unlimited supply. Every time you place an order with your words, it says "Yes, and would you like to supersize that?"

After all, if a former crack addict with a six-figure IRS debt can learn to speak the language of wealth fluently enough to manifest Caribbean living, you can too. Just remember - watch your mouth. The universe is listening, and it takes orders very literally.

Chapter 9
LIVING IN ABUNDANCE

Setting Prosperity Goals

You know what's harder than learning to talk abundance? Actually living it. Trust me, I know the difference. I spent years being the prosperity equivalent of someone who learns French from textbooks but freezes up when they actually visit Paris. I could speak the language of wealth, sure, but walking the walk? That was a whole other level of transformation.

I'm reminded of a moment in my office, about six months after I'd started really practicing this prosperity consciousness stuff. Vision boards covered my walls - the kind I used to make during my mortgage broker days, filled with images of beach houses, exotic vacations and the perfect soul mate. But something was different now. These weren't just pretty pictures anymore; they were possibilities I could feel in my bones.

That's what this chapter is about - the moment when prosperity consciousness stops being a concept and becomes your lived reality. When your goals aren't just wishes on paper but declarations to the universe that you're ready to play a bigger game.

We've learned to speak the language of wealth. Now it's time to set prosperity goals that make your inner critic gasp and your soul sing. It's time to create intentions so clear they practically manifest themselves instantaneously. Most importantly, it's time to become the person who naturally attracts and maintains abundance, rather than someone who's always chasing it.

Don't worry - I'm not going to hand you some cookie-cutter goal-setting formula or make you write SMART goals (though if you're into that sort of thing, more power to you). Instead, I'm going to show you how to dream bigger than you've ever allowed yourself before, set intentions that align with your soul's purpose, and take inspired action that feels more like flowing than forcing.

Ready to turn your prosperity consciousness into your prosperity reality? Let's begin with the first step: learning to dream bigger than you think possible...

Dream Bigger Than You Think Possible

Before we dive in, let's talk about this whole "goal" thing. You know how sometimes you learn a language just so you can explain to people in that country that you actually speak a different one? That's how I feel about goals. The corporate world understands goals. Vision board workshops talk about goals. But what I've discovered through years of manifestation - both the epic failures and the mind-blowing successes - is that the real magic happens when we shift from rigid goals to fluid intentions.

Here's the difference: Goals are like trying to navigate to a specific address. Intentions are like setting your internal GPS to "somewhere amazing" and trusting the journey. Both can get you somewhere good, but one leaves a lot more room for the universe to surprise you with something better than you could have planned.

I learned this lesson the expensive way. During my mortgage broker days, I was the queen of goal-setting. My office walls looked like a vision board factory exploded - specific income targets, precise timelines, exact models of cars I wanted. And sure, I managed to hit a lot of those targets. But you know where all that precise manifestation got me? Exactly what I asked for - no more, no less. It was like ordering from a menu without ever discovering what the chef's special might be.

Then cancer happened. Talk about a plot twist. Suddenly, all my carefully structured goals went out the window. I couldn't control my healing timeline. I couldn't force my body into compliance with my plans. For the first time in my life, I had to surrender to something bigger than my own agenda.

That's when I discovered the power of dreaming bigger by letting go of how those dreams would manifest. Instead of setting a goal of "pay for cancer treatment by X date," I held the intention of "experiencing complete healing and using this journey to serve others." The difference was profound. Not only did the resources for my treatment appear (in ways I never could have planned), but that intention expanded into teaching and helping others in ways my goal-oriented mind would never have imagined.

Let me tell you about the first time I really got this. I was sitting in my tiny apartment during my food stamp days, eating a dinner that cost less than my former drug habit would burn through in five minutes. Usually, this would be prime time for my inner critic to remind me of all my "realistic" limitations. But something was different. Instead of setting goals about getting off food stamps, I allowed myself to dream about creating prosperity consciousness so profound it would transform not just my life but thousands of others.

Was this "realistic"? About as realistic as a former crack addict with a six-figure IRS debt ending up teaching prosperity principles in the Caribbean. But here's what I've learned: The universe doesn't check your resume before granting your dreams. It doesn't care about your past. It only responds to your energetic frequency in the present moment.

This isn't about making vision boards with bigger houses or fancier cars (though if that's part of your dream, go for it). It's about expanding your conception of what's possible. When I started dreaming beyond my logical mind's limitations, something fascinating happened: The dreams themselves began showing me who I needed to become to manifest them.

Think about it - does an acorn set a goal to become an oak tree of specific dimensions? No, it holds the intention of fully expressing its oak tree nature and lets the elements determine the details. Your dreams are like that acorn - they contain everything needed for their fulfillment, if you'll just give them space to grow beyond your current understanding of what's possible.

The thing about self-imposed ceilings is that they're invisible until you smack your head against them. During my recovery journey, I kept hitting these ceilings I didn't even know I had. The first time I manifested six figures to settle part of my IRS debt, it blew my mind. Not because I'd never seen that kind of money before - I used to burn through more than that in my addiction days. No, what shocked me was discovering that if I could solve a six-figure problem, what else was possible?

Each ceiling I broke through revealed another level of possibility. It was like one of those video games where beating one level unlocks the next, except instead of fighting digital dragons, I was battling my own limiting beliefs. Resolving my IRS debt showed me six-figure problems were solvable. This led to creating six-figure solutions. Then multiple six figures. Then... why stop there?

Let me share something wild about breaking through these ceilings. Remember that hospital stay during my cancer treatment? One morning, a nurse brought me an extra blanket without me asking. My old self would have hoarded that blanket (yes, I actually used to try smuggling hospital blankets - not my proudest moment). But something had shifted. Instead of operating from scarcity, I found myself dreaming about having enough abundance to ensure every patient had all the comfort they needed.

That's the thing about dreams - they're contagious. Once you break through one ceiling, you start seeing ceilings everywhere, not just in your life but in how you imagine helping others. It's like getting upgraded to first class and instead of just enjoying the legroom, you start dreaming about how to make that experience accessible to everyone. Here's an exercise that transformed my own ability to dream bigger. I call it the Imagination Activation (honestly, it's more like giving your imagination permission to come out and play). Start by remembering something you've already achieved that once seemed impossible. For me, it was staying clean that first year. Every day without drugs seemed like a miracle. Now it's my new normal.

See how that achievement became your new baseline? That's how dreams work. Your current "impossible" dreams are just your next normal waiting to be realized. When I first imagined living part-time in the Caribbean, it seemed as likely as me becoming an astronaut (though given my expanding sense of possibility, don't rule that out either). But instead of dismissing it as impossible, I let myself fully feel it. What would that freedom feel like? How would that version of me move through the world? What kind of impact could I have from that place?

Let's talk about permission - not the kind you need from others, but the permission you need to give yourself. Here's what I discovered: You don't need to know HOW your biggest dreams will manifest. That's not your job. Your job is to stay open to possibilities your logical mind can't even conceive yet.

Look at nature - it's constantly demonstrating unlimited potential. Does a tree check its bank account before deciding whether to grow another branch? Does the ocean worry about containing too many waves? Does a hummingbird calculate the aerodynamics of what it's attempting? Nature dreams big by default, and last time I checked, we're part of nature.

I developed what I call the Dream Expansion Practice. Take your current biggest dream and multiply it by ten. Feel that resistance coming up? That's not your intuition warning you to be realistic - it's your consciousness showing you where it needs to expand. When I first dreamed of teaching prosperity principles, my vision was local workshops. When I multiplied that by ten, it became international teaching. When I multiplied that by ten again... well, let's just say the universe loves a good challenge.

This isn't just magical thinking. Quantum physics shows us that consciousness shapes reality. When I learned that our heart's electromagnetic field extends several feet beyond our body, literally affecting the physical world around us, it all clicked. By dreaming bigger, we're actually expanding our field of possibility.

Remember: The universe doesn't have a limit on your prosperity. Only you do. And those limits? They're just stories waiting to be rewritten.

Speaking of expanding possibilities - let me tell you about the moment this really clicked. I was sitting in a coffee shop in Playa del Carmen, sipping an overpriced latte and feeling a bit guilty about the expense, when a group of digital nomads at the next table caught my attention. They were talking about running their businesses from anywhere in the world, and I heard myself think, "Must be nice."

That phrase stopped me cold. "Must be nice" had been my go-to response for other people's success stories back in my addiction days. It was the language of someone watching life instead of living it. Right there, between sips of my fancy coffee, I pulled out my journal and wrote: "What if I could teach prosperity principles anywhere in the world?"

That single question expanded into a vision so much bigger than my original "maybe I'll do some local workshops" plan. Within months, I was teaching internationally. Within a year, I had created a life that moved between Texas and the Caribbean. Not because I'm special, but because I finally gave my dreams permission to outgrow my fears.

From Impossible Dreams to Reality

Here's what nobody tells you about transforming impossible dreams into reality: The bridge between them isn't built with vision boards and affirmations (though those are nice accessories). It's built with a fascinating blend of quantum physics, heart coherence, and what I like to call "divine audacity."

Let me explain. During my darkest days of IRS debt, I attended a seminar where they talked about the HeartMath Institute's research on heart coherence. They explained how our heart's electromagnetic field extends several feet beyond our body, literally affecting the physical world around us. The scientist in me was skeptical, but the former crack addict who'd manifested money out of nowhere during my using days thought, "Well, that explains a few things."

What I discovered in transforming my own impossible dreams into reality was something I wish they'd taught me in all those corporate goal-setting workshops: Your heart's intelligence is actually way ahead of your brain's careful planning. While your mind is busy making spreadsheets and timelines, your heart is already communicating with the quantum field of infinite possibilities.

Sounds woo-woo? I thought so too, until I started putting it into practice. Remember my "random" urge to call that tax attorney who ended up helping me settle my IRS debt? That wasn't my logical brain's idea - it was my heart's intelligence picking up signals my mind couldn't compute. Scientists call this "non-local intuition." I call it my inner GPS to miracles.

During my cancer journey, I had plenty of time in that hospital bed to study the science behind manifestation. Turns out, quantum physicists have a name for what happens when we focus our attention on potential outcomes - they call it "the observer effect." Every time you observe a possibility, you're literally affecting its likelihood of manifesting. Who knew all those hours I spent visualizing my Caribbean teaching life were actually shifting quantum probabilities?

But here's what changed everything for me: Understanding that manifesting isn't about forcing outcomes - it's about aligning your heart's field with what you want to create. Think of it like tuning a radio. You don't have to build the radio station or generate the music. You just have to tune to the right frequency.

I remember the exact moment this clicked. I was doing my usual morning meditation (which back then mostly consisted of trying not to think about all the things I should be doing instead of meditating). Suddenly, I felt this profound sense of peace - not about achieving my dreams, but about who I was becoming in pursuit of them. It was like the universe whispered, "Honey, you've been pushing when you should have been allowing."

The shift from pushing to allowing changed everything. Instead of forcing my international teaching dreams into a five-year plan, I started paying attention to what brought me alive. When an opportunity to speak at a small workshop in Costa Rica appeared, my logical mind said "You can't afford that." But my heart was already packing its bags.

The key is what I call "coherent dreaming" - where your heart's wisdom and your soul's vision align with universal timing. It's like hitting the sweet spot in manifestation, where synchronicities start popping up like those whack-a-mole games at carnivals, except instead of plastic moles, it's opportunities you couldn't have planned better if you tried.

Want to know something wild? The HeartMath researchers found that your heart actually receives information about future events before they happen. They call it "precognition." I call it proof that your heart already knows the path to your dreams. Your job isn't to figure everything out - it's to get your overthinking brain out of the way long enough to let your heart lead.

This isn't just spiritual theory - it's backed by science. When you're in a state of heart coherence, your body's systems synchronize, your brain functions better, and you literally become a more powerful attractor of opportunities. It's like upgrading your manifestation hardware from dial-up to high-speed fiber optic.

Let me give you a concrete example of coherent dreaming in action. During my first year of international teaching, I had this wild vision of hosting retreats in Mexico. But instead of jumping straight into planning mode (my old approach which usually involved spreadsheets, panic attacks, and late-night chocolate chip binges), I tried something different.

Every morning, I'd sit in what I called my "heart space" - usually my bedroom floor with a cup of coffee, nothing fancy. Instead of visualizing the perfect venue or ideal number of participants, I'd feel into the energy of what I wanted to create. How would it feel to guide transformations in paradise? What would my participants experience? What version of me needed to emerge to make this real?

Here's where it gets interesting. One morning during this practice, I felt an inexplicable urge to go to a specific cafe in Texas - not my usual spot. There, I "randomly" met someone who owned a retreat center in Playa del Carmen. But here's the kicker - if I'd been forcing my original vision of how the Mexico retreats should look, I might have missed this completely different door the universe was opening.

This is what I mean by allowing versus forcing. The universe's GPS often takes some interesting detours. While my logical mind was trying to figure out how to market retreats in Mexico, the quantum field was already arranging a "chance" meeting that would lead to something even better.

The science nerds among you (and yes, despite my questionable life choices, I'm secretly one of them) might appreciate this: Stanford researchers found that the heart's electromagnetic field is about 5,000 times stronger than the brain's. Think about that. While your brain is busy making pro/con lists, your heart is broadcasting your deepest intentions to the universe with the power of a spiritual radio tower.

But you want to know the real secret? The magic happens when you stop trying to control the "how." During my drug days, I could manifest money like a magician pulling rabbits from a hat - not because I had a detailed plan, but because my desperation created a kind of laser-focused intention. Now imagine applying that same intensity of focus to something that actually serves your highest good. That's coherent dreaming.

I remember sitting in my first international workshop, watching participants have breakthrough after breakthrough, and thinking, "This is better than anything I could have planned." And it was. Because it wasn't just my plan - it was the result of aligning my heart's wisdom with universal intelligence.

This is where most manifestation teachings miss the mark. They focus on the "what" - what you want to create, what you want to have, what you want to achieve. But the real power lies in the "who" - who you're becoming in pursuit of your dreams. Every impossible dream that becomes reality transforms both the dream and the dreamer.

That transformation from dreamer to manifestor brings us to something nobody talks about in those perky morning motivational videos - the messy middle part where you have to become someone bigger than your current story.

Take my Caribbean life, for example. Before it manifested physically, I had to become the kind of person who could sustain that reality. It wasn't just about having enough money - it was about expanding my consciousness to match the size of the dream. Trust me, moving between Texas and paradise requires a way bigger version of yourself than hiding from the IRS does.

I learned this lesson during what I call my "fake it till you feel it" phase. There I was, still living on food stamps but teaching prosperity principles (talk about imposter syndrome having a field day). One morning, during my coffee-and-coherence practice, I had this insight that hit me harder than my first hit of crack: I wasn't supposed to wait until I had millions to be the person who could handle millions. I needed to be that person now.

That's when I started what I now call "living from the future self backward." Instead of pushing toward some distant goal, I began making decisions as if I were already the international teacher and prosperity guide I envisioned becoming. Here's the wild part - the moment I shifted into being that version of me, opportunities started showing up that would have seemed impossible to my old self.

But let's get real for a minute. This isn't about pretending to be something you're not. Lord knows I tried that approach during my addiction years, and all it got me was an Oscar-worthy performance of "functional addict who totally has it together" (spoiler alert: nobody was buying it). This is about recognizing who you truly are beneath all the stories and limitations you've accumulated.

This understanding changed everything about how I set intentions - which, by the way, are worlds apart from traditional goal-setting. While goals live in the land of "someday," intentions reside in the eternal now. They're less about achieving and more about becoming.

You know that moment in The Wizard of Oz when Dorothy realizes she had the power to go home all along? I had a similar epiphany during one of my prosperity workshops. I was teaching about manifestation when a participant, Mary Beth, asked the question that changed everything: "How do I know if I'm setting goals or just making wishes?"

The room got quiet, like it does when someone finally asks the thing everyone's thinking. I found myself sharing a truth I'd learned the hard way: Goals without aligned intentions are just pretty wishes taped to your bathroom mirror. But intentions? They're like spiritual DNA - they contain everything needed to create your reality.

Looking back at my own journey - from crack houses to Caribbean beaches, from IRS nightmares to international teaching - I realized something profound. The times I'd truly manifested transformation weren't when I was pushing toward goals. They were when I'd set crystal clear intentions that resonated with who I was becoming.

Creating Clear Intentions

Let me tell you about the difference between goals and intentions, and why it matters more than what color Post-it notes you use for your vision board. During my mortgage broker days, I was the queen of goal setting. I could write SMART goals that would make any corporate trainer weep with joy. I had numbers, timelines, action steps - the whole enchilada. And sure, I hit a lot of those targets. I also hit rock bottom with clockwork precision.

Here's what nobody tells you in those goal-setting workshops: Intentions operate at a quantum level where energy precedes matter. I know, I know - sounds like something you'd hear at a crystal shop in Sedona. But stick with me here. When I was working with my first spiritual teacher (who, by the way, had to put up with me showing up to meditation still buzzing from the night before), she said something that finally made this click.

"Debbie," she said, with that patience only spiritual teachers and kindergarten teachers seem to master, "you're trying to force the universe to follow your schedule. How's that working out for you?"

It wasn't. I was still approaching my spiritual transformation like a corporate project plan. Three months to enlightenment, six months to financial freedom, one year to total life transformation - with quarterly reviews and PowerPoint presentations. The universe, it turns out, doesn't really care about your Gantt chart.

But intentions? They're different. They operate more like a frequency you tune into rather than a destination you're trying to reach. Think of it like this: During my addiction years, I could manifest money for drugs with uncanny precision. Not because I had a detailed plan (trust me, addicts aren't known for their strategic planning skills), but because my entire being was aligned with that intention. The universe doesn't judge our intentions - it just responds to their clarity and power.

I remember the exact moment this shifted for me. I was sitting in my tiny apartment during my food stamp days, writing what I thought was another goal list. Instead of my usual "Make X dollars by Y date," I wrote something different: "I am someone who creates and sustains abundant wealth to serve others." It wasn't a goal - it was a declaration of identity. Not something to achieve, but someone to become.

That simple shift changed everything. Instead of pushing toward external targets, I started aligning my energy with this new identity. Rather than saying "I want to be debt-free," I began living as someone who was already in harmony with universal flow. The IRS didn't immediately disappear (wouldn't that have been nice?), but solutions started appearing in ways my goal-oriented mind could never have planned.

Here's what's wild: The universe responds to who you're being, not what you're chasing. During my cancer journey, I stopped setting goals about healing timelines and started holding the intention of being fully alive in each moment. Not only did this transform my healing process, but it opened doors I didn't even know existed.

Let me share something that revolutionized my understanding of intentions versus goals. During my international teaching, I noticed something fascinating: The students who created the most dramatic transformations weren't the ones with the most detailed goal lists or the fanciest vision boards. They were the ones who fundamentally shifted who they were being.

Take Margaret, one of my students from Los Angeles. She came to my workshop with a meticulously planned goal to double her income in six months. Very SMART goal, very corporate, very impressive. But she was still being the person who needed to prove her worth through achievement. During our work together, she shifted to the intention of "being someone who creates value effortlessly." Notice the difference? Goals are about doing. Intentions are about being.

Within three months, she'd not only doubled her income but had created opportunities she couldn't have planned for. Why? Because she'd shifted her energy from chasing to attracting, from pushing to allowing.

I learned this lesson myself during what I call my "surrender summer" - that period after my cancer treatment when I was living on food stamps and had exactly zero control over how my future would unfold. Instead of my usual goal of "make X amount by doing Y," I held the intention of being a channel for prosperity consciousness. Period. No timeline, no specific dollar amount, no detailed how-to plan.

The results? Let's just say the universe has a much better imagination than your vision board. Teaching opportunities appeared from nowhere. My first international invitation arrived out of the blue. The Caribbean connection manifested through a "random" coffee shop encounter. None of these were on my goal list because my limited mind couldn't have conceived them.

But here's what really cooked my noodle: The universe doesn't just respond to your conscious intentions. It responds to your energetic truth. During my mortgage broker days, I could set all the income goals I wanted, but as long as I was being someone who didn't believe she deserved lasting wealth, guess what? The money would come and go faster than a chocolate cake at a Weight Watchers meeting.

Let me share how I learned to create intentions that the universe actually takes seriously. It's like placing an order at a cosmic restaurant - you've got to speak clearly and mean what you say, or you might end up with something very different from what you had in mind.

During my early recovery days, I set what I thought was a clear intention: "I want to be financially stable." Sounds good, right? Except "stable" to my subconscious mind (which had a pretty twisted relationship with money) meant "just enough to survive." And that's exactly what I got - bare minimum stability.

The universe, being the efficient delivery service it is, gave me exactly what my energy was ordering.

Here's how I learned to create intentions that actually work. Instead of "I want to be financially stable," I shifted to "I am someone who creates and sustains abundant wealth." Instead of "I want to help people," I became "I am a powerful channel for transformation." Feel the difference? The first version comes from lack. The second comes from wholeness. But let me tell you about my favorite intention disaster - it's like the cosmic equivalent of ordering diet coke and getting a milkshake. Back in Texas, I set the intention to "attract more clients." Boy, did the universe have fun with that one. I got more clients alright - the kind that drained my energy, haggled over prices, and made me question my life choices. I hadn't been specific about the quality of clients or the kind of work I wanted to do. It's like telling the universe "surprise me" and then being shocked when it does.

That taught me what I call the "Be-Do-Have" principle of intention setting. Most people go about it backwards. They think, "Once I have money, I'll do great things, and then I'll be successful." But the universe works in reverse: You need to be the person who naturally does those things, and then you'll have the results that person would have.

For example, when I was dreaming about teaching internationally, I stopped setting goals about making it happen. Instead, I started being an international teacher right where I was. I shifted how I presented myself, how I structured my material, how I thought about my work. The physical reality of teaching abroad followed naturally - because I was already being that person energetically.

Here's a truth that transformed how I set intentions: Your intention has to match who you're being in this moment. I remember sitting in my first prosperity workshop after cancer, teaching about abundance while technically being broke. But instead of feeling like a fraud, I was fully being someone who understood and embodied prosperity principles. The money followed that being-ness, not the other way around.

Let me share the exact moment this crystallized for me. I was doing my morning practice - which at the time consisted of coffee, journal, and trying not to freak out about bills - when I wrote this intention: "I am someone who naturally attracts perfect opportunities." Not very specific, right? But here's the key: I started being that person immediately. When an invitation to speak at a small local event came up, I treated it with the same professional excellence I would give a TED talk.

That small event led to bigger ones, which led to international opportunities, which led to... well, you get the picture. But none of that would have happened if I'd stayed stuck in planning mode instead of moving into inspired action.

And that's really what separates wishful thinking from real transformation - the ability to act from inspiration rather than desperation. Speaking of which, let me tell you about the day I learned the difference between forced action and inspired action. It involves a "random" trip to a coffee shop that changed everything...

Picture this: I'm sitting in my favorite coffee shop in Texas, journaling about my intentions like the good spiritual student I was trying to be. A voice inside (the same one that used to tell me where to score drugs, now divinely repurposed) says, "Go to the other coffee shop across town." My logical mind argues - I'm comfortable here, my latte's still half full, and did I mention I'm comfortable here?

But there was something different about this nudge. It wasn't the frantic energy of my old goal-chasing days. It wasn't my addiction-driven desperation. It was softer, clearer, like a cosmic GPS saying "recalculating route."

Now, in my former life, I was the queen of forced action. Need money? Make calls until someone says yes. Want to grow the business? Work longer hours. Everything was push, push, push. And it worked... sort of. Like using a sledgehammer to open a jar of pickles - you might get it open, but there's going to be mess everywhere.

This felt different. It was what I now recognize as inspired action - the kind that feels more like being moved by grace than pushing against resistance. So I did something my old self would have found ridiculous: I packed up my half-full latte and drove across town.

That "random" coffee shop visit led to meeting someone who would later become instrumental in launching my international teaching career. But here's what's fascinating - if I'd gone there with an agenda, desperately networking or trying to make something happen, I probably would have missed the connection entirely.

The thing about divine nudges is that they don't come with flashing neon signs saying "THIS IS YOUR COSMIC GPS SPEAKING." Sometimes they show up as a quiet knowing, sometimes as a random thought that won't leave you alone, and sometimes - my personal favorite - as what I call a "holy homework assignment."

Let me tell you about one of these assignments. I was teaching a prosperity workshop in Italy, when I felt this undeniable urge to share a particularly embarrassing story about my crack cocaine days. My ego was screaming "Don't you dare! You're supposed to be a respected teacher!" But there was that nudge again.

So I shared the story - about how I once manifested money for drugs faster than most people could order a pizza. But instead of just leaving it at the cringe-worthy parts, I connected it to how the same manifesting power that had once fueled my addiction was now creating international teaching opportunities. The room got so quiet you could hear a paradigm shift.

After the workshop, a woman approached me in tears. Turned out she was struggling with her own addiction, hiding it behind a successful corporate career, just like I used to. That vulnerable share led to a transformation that logic could never have planned. This is what inspired action looks like - it often makes no sense until you look back and see the divine orchestration.

But here's what nobody tells you about inspired action: Sometimes it looks like doing nothing. During my cancer treatment, there were days when the inspired action was simply to rest. My achievement-oriented mind hated this. It wanted to be working on my next program, writing my book, doing something "productive." The truly inspired action was to allow myself to heal.

I remember lying in that hospital bed, feeling like a failure because I wasn't "making things happen." Then one of my nurses said something that changed everything: "Maybe the universe needs you to be still long enough to receive what's next." Talk about a holy two-by-four upside the head.

Learning to distinguish between ego-driven action and divine nudges is like developing a new sense - call it your spiritual Spidey sense. During my early recovery days, I kept confusing desperation with inspiration. You know that feeling when you're trying to convince yourself something is a "sign from the universe" but really it's just your old patterns dressed up in spiritual sheep's clothing?

Here's a perfect example: Decades ago, shortly after getting clean, I felt what I thought was an "inspired nudge" to start a business venture with another recovering addict. My ego dressed it up as "helping another person in recovery" but really, it was my old hustler energy looking for a fix of success. How could I tell? Because the energy felt frantic, urgent, like I had to make it happen right now or the opportunity would vanish.

True inspired action has a completely different flavor. It feels more like being pulled by joy than pushed by fear. When I got the nudge to write this book, it didn't come with a side of anxiety. Even when my inner critic was throwing a full-on tantrum about my qualifications (or lack thereof), there was this underlying sense of rightness that felt like floating rather than swimming upstream.

Let me share my favorite "divine nudge vs. ego drive" moment. I was in Playa del Carmen, supposedly on vacation but still checking emails compulsively (because apparently my ego thought the universe would stop spinning without my constant attention). I felt this gentle urge to put my phone away and walk on the beach. My ego immediately protested: "But what about that important client email? What about the workshop you need to plan? What about...?"

But there was that floating feeling again. So I did something radical - I left my phone in my room. During that "unproductive" beach walk, I had the clearest download about how to restructure my entire teaching program. The inspiration that came while I was "doing nothing" was better than anything I could have forced through hours of strategic planning.

This is what I mean by trusting divine timing. Your ego wants to make things happen on its schedule. The universe has its own timeline, and let me tell you something I learned the hard way - its timing is way better than yours.

Here's my foolproof test for distinguishing divine timing from ego panic: If it feels like you're trying to push the river, it's ego. If it feels like you're riding the current, it's inspiration. During my mortgage broker days, I was constantly pushing the river - making deals happen through sheer force of will. The money came, sure, but it never stayed because I was operating outside of divine flow.

Now I know better. When I get an inspired nudge, I do what I call the "body check." My ego might be jumping up and down with excitement or anxiety, but what's happening in my body? Is there a sense of expansion or contraction? Are my shoulders up around my ears, or am I breathing easily? The body never lies.

Just last week, I got what seemed like an amazing opportunity to speak at a prestigious event. My ego was doing cartwheels, but my body felt like it was wearing a corset three sizes too small. Sure enough, when I politely declined, a much better opportunity - one that aligned perfectly with my current teaching - showed up two days later.

This is the art of inspired action - learning to trust the subtle signals over the loud demands of ego. It's about recognizing that sometimes the most powerful action is stillness, and sometimes the smallest step, taken in alignment, creates bigger ripples than all our frantic swimming. Speaking of ripples... let me show you a powerful tool that brings together everything we've talked about - dreaming bigger, setting clear intentions, and following inspired action. It's called Your Prosperity Vision Board, but trust me, this isn't your typical "paste pictures of sports cars on cardboard" exercise. This is about creating a visual representation of who you're becoming.

Before you go running for the glue sticks and old magazines, let me tell you why most vision boards are pushing rather than allowing. Sure they work but not as spectacularly as they could sometimes not at all. Remember when I told you about my mortgage-broker-days vision board? It was plastered with photos of beach houses and spa treatments - basically a high-end shopping catalog masquerading as manifestation. And guess what? I actually manifested some of those things. Then promptly lost them because I was focused on the stuff rather than who I needed to become.

Here's what changed everything. After my cancer journey, I was sitting in my tiny apartment, ready to create a new vision board. But instead of reaching for pictures of material success, I felt this nudge (you know, those divine ones we just talked about) to do something different. Rather than collecting images of what I wanted to have, I started gathering images that represented who I wanted to be.

Let me share a secret about vision boards that nobody talks about: The universe doesn't respond to the pictures - it responds to the energy they activate in you. During my addiction days, I could manifest money for drugs because my entire being was aligned with that intention. The same principle works with vision boards, but here's the key - they need to resonate with your soul, not just your wish list.

I remember finding this image of a wise older woman teaching under a tree. Nothing glamorous, nothing flashy, but something in that picture spoke to the teacher I wanted to become. It ended up in the center of my board, surrounded not by symbols of wealth, but by representations of wisdom, impact, and joy. That board became less about accumulating and more about becoming.

Let me walk you through the process that transformed my own vision boarding from a glorified wish list into a powerful tool for transformation. First, forget everything you learned in those manifestation workshops about creating the perfect board. This isn't about making it look pretty - it's about making it feel true.

I learned this lesson during a workshop I was teaching in Alaska. A participant had created this gorgeous vision board - professionally designed, perfectly arranged, looked like something from a Pinterest board. But when I asked her how it made her feel, she admitted, "Like I'm looking at someone else's life." Bingo.

Here's what I do now, and what I teach my students. Before you even think about picking up a magazine, create what I call your "sacred space setup." For me, this means coffee (obviously), my favorite music playing softly, and usually some form of chocolate within arm's reach. This isn't just about being comfortable - it's about creating an environment where your inner wisdom can speak louder than your inner critic.

I remember the first time I did this new approach. I was sitting on my floor in Texas, surrounded by magazines, when I realized I was about to do my old pattern - looking for the flashiest, most impressive images. Instead, I put everything down, closed my eyes, and asked myself, "Who am I becoming?" The answer brought tears to my eyes, and not one of the images it brought to mind involved a sports car.

The board I created that day had some unusual choices. There was a picture of hands holding soil - representing my connection to being grounded in truth.

An image of a laughing elderly couple - embodying the joy I wanted to teach from. A photograph of a pristine, empty beach at sunrise - symbolizing the peace I wanted to emanate, not just experience. The most powerful image on that board wasn't even particularly spiritual - it was a picture of a battered coffee cup. See, every morning during my recovery, I'd practice gratitude with my coffee, treating each sip like it was served in fine china, even when I was using a chipped mug from the dollar store. That coffee cup represented who I was becoming - someone who could find abundance in every moment, not just the Instagram-worthy ones.

Here's another secret about deep vision boarding - sometimes the perfect images find you. I was once desperately searching magazines for pictures that represented "international teacher" when my niece brought me a drawing she'd made of a butterfly emerging from its cocoon. That crude crayon drawing captured exactly who I was becoming better than any polished magazine photo could have.

Let me show you how to create your own transformation vision board - one that actually works because it's aligned with your soul's evolution, not just your wish list.

First, create your sacred space. This isn't woo-woo optional stuff - it's about getting quiet enough to hear your inner wisdom. Put on music that makes your soul dance (mine's usually a mix of zen meditation and 70s funk, because why choose?). Light a candle if that's your thing. Get comfortable but stay alert - this isn't nap time, even though my first few attempts definitely ended in drool.

Before you touch a single magazine or open Pinterest, sit quietly with these questions:

Who am I becoming as I step into my prosperity consciousness?
What energy do I want to embody?
How do I want people to feel in my presence?
What truth am I here to express?

Write down whatever comes without censoring. During my first time doing this, I wrote "joyful prosperity teacher" and immediately heard my inner critic laugh. Write it down anyway.

Now, when you start collecting images, look for ones that make your soul hum. Not your ego - your soul. There's a difference. Your ego wants the mansion photo. Your soul might be more drawn to the image of an open door or an ancient tree. Trust that magnetic pull.

Here's the technical part:

- Get a board that feels good to touch (this matters - you'll be working with it daily)
- Gather magazines, but also collect things that carry meaning - tickets from meaningful events, leaves from powerful moments, anything that holds energy for you
- Create three sections on your board: Being, Becoming, Beyond
- Being is who you are now when you're most aligned
- Becoming is who you're growing into
- Beyond is what's possible that you can't even imagine yet

When you're arranging your images, forget about making it look perfect. My first transformation board had gaps and overlaps and wasn't going to win any design awards. But it was real, and that's what made it powerful.

The final step - and this is crucial - is to write an activation statement for your board. Mine was "I am the living embodiment of prosperity consciousness, teaching through my being more than my words." Place this at the bottom of your board as a foundation for everything above it. Use your board daily, but not like a cosmic shopping list. Instead of staring at it making wishes, step into it. Feel yourself becoming what those images represent. Let it remind you of who you really are beneath all the stories and limitations.

Remember: This isn't about creating a picture-perfect future. It's about recognizing and becoming the person who naturally attracts your deepest dreams - not because you're trying to get something, but because you're finally allowing yourself to be who you truly are.

Your vision board should make you catch your breath a little. If it doesn't scare you and excite you in equal measure, you might be playing too small. Dream bigger. Reach deeper. Be bolder in claiming who you're becoming.

This is your permission slip to create something that reflects your soul's truth, not society's expectations. Make it weird. Make it wonderful. Make it absolutely, authentically you.

Chapter 10

MAINTAINING THE ABUNDANCE MINDSET

The email notification pinged. Another unexpected bill. You know that moment when your stomach drops and your throat tightens? That used to be my default response to any financial surprise. But something was different now. Instead of launching into my familiar panic dance (which usually involved avoiding my bank balance believing it might magically change), I felt myself take a deep breath. This is what maintaining an abundance mindset looks like in real life - not the Instagram version, but the messy, beautiful reality of it.

Dealing with Setbacks and Fear

Let me tell you about the moment I really learned how to handle setbacks. I was lying in a hospital bed the day after Christmas, getting blood transfusions just to stay alive. My body was so weak I could barely lift my head off the pillow. That's when my phone rang with the news that would test every prosperity principle I'd ever taught.

My primary client - actually, my only client at the time - was firing me. Not because of poor performance. Not because of the cancer. But because his wife suspected we were having an affair. The irony would have been hilarious if it wasn't so terrifying - I could barely make it to the bathroom by myself, let alone engage in some imagined romantic intrigue. In that moment, everything I'd learned about abundance consciousness faced its ultimate test. I wasn't just dealing with a health crisis - I was staring at complete financial ruin. Food stamps loomed in my future. The fear wasn't just knocking at my door; it was trying to move in and redecorate.

Here's what most prosperity teachers won't tell you: Sometimes your abundance consciousness gets stripped down to its bare bones. It's not pretty. It's not Pinterest-worthy. It's you, alone in a hospital bed, choosing between bitterness and blessing.

I could have done what my old self would have - spiral into victim mode, curse the universe, maybe even start plotting ways to dramatically expose my client's wife's paranoia (hey, I had a lot of time lying in that hospital bed to scheme). Instead, I found myself doing something that surprised me. I started laughing.

Not because it was funny, but because in that moment, I finally got it. This wasn't just another setback - it was an invitation to demonstrate everything I'd been teaching about prosperity consciousness. Talk about a cosmic pop quiz.

The real test came when my doctor walked in right after that phone call. He had that look - you know the one, where they're trying to decide whether to give you the bad news with or without sugar coating. My CT scan showed a spot on my liver and he recommended a PET Scan. Insurance was nonexistent and I certainly did not have the funds to pay for the PET Scan. And now, with my only client firing me, I had no idea how I'd pay for any treatments regardless. My savings were dwindling faster than sands through an hourglass.

This was what I call a "choice point" moment. We all have them - those crossroads where we either cave to fear or choose something bigger. It's like that moment in my addiction when I had to choose between the familiar comfort of getting high and the terrifying unknown of getting clean.

You want to know the real difference between temporary abundance and unshakeable prosperity consciousness? It's not about never feeling fear - it's about what you do with that fear when it shows up. It's like what I learned during my drug user days: the same energy that could manifest money for drugs could be redirected toward something greater. Fear is just energy waiting to be redirected.

I made a decision in that hospital bed that changed everything. Instead of focusing on what I was losing, I started focusing on what I was learning. Instead of seeing myself as a victim of circumstance, I began seeing myself as a student of transformation. Every setback became a setup for a comeback.

This isn't some Pollyanna "everything happens for a reason" nonsense. Sometimes things happen because life is messy and unpredictable. But you always have a choice about what meaning you assign to those events. We create every story we tell ourselves.

What happened next taught me something profound about prosperity consciousness that I couldn't have learned any other way. I call it the Phoenix Principle - sometimes life strips everything away so you can discover that your prosperity consciousness isn't dependent on external circumstances.

During that year of healing, I experienced what I now call "intentional poverty." Living on food stamps, tracking every penny, I made a shocking discovery: I was happier with nothing than I'd been with everything. Not because poverty is fun (trust me, dollar store Christmas cookies aren't anyone's idea of abundance), but because I finally understood that prosperity isn't about what you have - it's about who you are.

The sacred economy of healing revealed itself during endless hours in doctors' offices. The surgeons had their own limiting story: "You'll have to live with an appliance on your stomach for the rest of your life." But I knew something deeper - the same consciousness that could heal my body could restore my finances. Both were simply different expressions of the same abundance principle.

That year taught me that:

Joy doesn't require resources (my happiest moments were sitting in silence with my morning coffee)
Peace isn't purchased (it comes from alignment, not acquisition)
Abundance is a state of being (not a state of bank account)
Healing follows consciousness (not the other way around)

Here's what's wild - within five years of that rock bottom moment, I had not only healed completely without the predicted permanent appliance, but I had created another million dollars. However (and this is crucial), this wasn't just about money returning. The real miracle was maintaining the consciousness I'd developed during my year of nothing.

The Five-Year Phoenix Rise wasn't just about financial recovery - it was about maintaining a completely new relationship with prosperity. During my deepest healing moments, when all I could do was rest and receive, I learned that every moment is pregnant with possibility. Even lying in that hospital bed, I could feel abundance flowing - in the kindness of nurses, in the sunlight streaming through my window, in the simple miracle of breath.

You might be thinking, "That's great for you, Debbie, but my challenges are different." I get it. Whether you're facing financial stress, health issues, or relationship struggles, the principle remains the same: your prosperity consciousness isn't determined by your circumstances.

How I Handle Challenges Now

These days, when something that looks like a setback appears, I have a completely different response system. Take that burst pipe in my Texas home while I was teaching in the Caribbean. Instead of my old pattern of panic and catastrophizing, I've developed what I call the "Sacred Response Protocol."

First, I acknowledge the reality of the situation without getting lost in the drama. Yes, there's water everywhere. Yes, it's a mess. Yes, this is going to require time and money to fix. But none of that dictates my prosperity consciousness.

Second, I look for what I call the "abundance opportunity." Every challenge carries within it the seed of greater prosperity - if you know how to look for it. That burst pipe? It led to a complete home renovation covered by insurance, something I'd been dreaming about but hadn't prioritized. More importantly, it connected me with a contractor who ended up joining my prosperity program and transforming his entire business model.

You can start practicing this same principle right now. Take your current biggest challenge - the one that's testing your prosperity consciousness the most. Instead of seeing it as evidence that prosperity principles don't work, ask yourself:

- What's the invitation in this situation?
- What consciousness is trying to emerge?
- How can this serve my growth?
- Where's the hidden opportunity?

In my drug addled days, I used to be able to manifest money for drugs with uncanny precision. That same manifestation power didn't disappear - it just got redirected toward something greater. Your challenges are similar - they're not evidence of lack, they're opportunities for redirecting your prosperity consciousness toward something bigger.

But here's what really shifted everything - I started documenting these transformations. Not just in my head, but in what I call my "Evidence Journal." Every time a seeming setback revealed itself as a setup for something better, I wrote it down. Why? Because our brains have spiritual amnesia when it comes to remembering how situations work out. We remember the crisis but forget the miracle.

Let me give you another example. Last year, I lost what I thought was a dream speaking opportunity - a major conference that would have put me in front of thousands. I felt that old familiar knot in my stomach, that "maybe I'm not good enough" voice trying to make a comeback tour in my head. But instead of spiraling, I opened my Evidence Journal.

There it was - the story of losing my only client while in the hospital, which led to creating my own programs that have reached far more people than that single client relationship ever could. The story of my IRS debt that seemed impossible to resolve, which became the foundation for teaching others about true prosperity. Pattern after pattern of divine redirection.

This isn't just positive thinking - it's practical prosperity consciousness in action. You can start your own Evidence Journal today. Every time something appears to go "wrong," document it. Then, keep updating that same entry as the situation unfolds. You'll start seeing patterns of how the universe is always working in your favor, even when it doesn't feel like it in the moment.

But here's the thing I discovered - trying to maintain this consciousness alone is like trying to swim upstream wearing concrete shoes. Which brings me to one of the most crucial elements of maintaining prosperity consciousness: creating support systems that actually enhance your abundance awareness rather than drain it.

Creating Support Systems

You want to know the biggest lie I told myself during my early prosperity journey? "I have to figure this out alone." Maybe it was leftover pride from my addiction days when asking for help felt like weakness. Or maybe it was that old achiever mindset that said success only counts if you do it solo.

Either way, I learned the hard way that isolation is actually a form of poverty consciousness. Think about it - believing you have to handle everything alone is just another version of "there's not enough." Not enough support, not enough connection, not enough community.

Let me share something that rocked my world recently. The U.S. Surgeon General declared loneliness an epidemic, saying it carries the same health risks as smoking fifteen cigarettes a day. When I share this in my workshops, people get uncomfortable - because deep down, we know we're all carrying some version of this isolation.

During my cancer journey, I noticed something fascinating. The patients who tried to battle cancer alone often struggled the most, not just physically but spiritually. Meanwhile, those of us who allowed ourselves to be supported - who created conscious communities around our healing - often experienced unexpected abundance even in the midst of crisis.

I remember the day everything shifted. I was sitting in my hospital room, trying to maintain my prosperity consciousness while feeling absolutely terrified. Sarah, my friend from my first prosperity workshop, walked in. Instead of the usual "you've got this" pep talk, she sat down and said something that changed everything: "You teach us about abundance, but you're living in scarcity of support."

That hit me like a spiritual two-by-four. Here I was, teaching prosperity principles while hoarding my struggles. Trying to maintain some perfect image of "prosperity teacher who never wobbles." Sarah's honesty cracked open something in me, and that's when I learned about what I now call "Conscious Community."

It's not just about having people around you - it's about having the right people around you. I call it your "Prosperity Posse." These aren't just cheerleaders who tell you what you want to hear. They're truth-tellers who hold space for your greatness even when you've temporarily forgotten it.

Let me give you an example. During my recovery, I created what I call my "Abundance Accountability Circle." Every Wednesday morning, rain or shine, four of us would meet at this tiny coffee shop. We had one rule: you had to share both a victory and a vulnerability. No pretending everything was perfect, but no staying stuck in the struggle either.

This wasn't your typical networking group or support circle. We were literally rewiring each other's prosperity consciousness through shared experience. When Magda shared how she turned a client rejection into a better opportunity, it strengthened my own ability to see setbacks as setups. When Marcus talked about maintaining abundance consciousness through his divorce, it showed me new possibilities for handling my own challenges.

You can start creating your own Prosperity Posse today. Look for people who:

Challenge your limiting stories with love
Celebrate your wins without competition
Hold space for your struggles without letting you camp there
Demonstrate prosperity consciousness in their own lives

But here's the crucial part - this isn't just about receiving support. It's about becoming a prosperity anchor for others. Some of my deepest abundance breakthroughs came when I was helping someone else maintain their prosperity consciousness through challenges.

Remember my contractor from the burst pipe story? He joined our Abundance Accountability Circle, thinking he was just going to learn about manifesting more business. Instead, he discovered how his own scarcity consciousness was affecting every area of his life. Now he's teaching other contractors about conscious business practices. That's how prosperity consciousness spreads - through community.

The ripple effect of conscious community showed me something crucial about maintaining prosperity consciousness - it requires consistent practice, not just crisis management. It's like what I learned in recovery: you don't wait until you're craving drugs to work your program. You build habits that keep you strong before the challenges hit.

I remember sharing this insight during one of our Wednesday morning circles. Marcus looked up from his coffee and said, "So you're telling me prosperity consciousness is like a muscle?" I laughed and said, "More like a whole gym membership - and you've got to show up regularly, not just when you're feeling motivated."

That conversation sparked what became one of my most powerful teachings about maintaining abundance mindset. Because here's what nobody tells you about prosperity consciousness - it's not just about what you do during the big moments. It's about the tiny choices you make every single day that either strengthen or weaken your abundance awareness.

Building Lasting Prosperity Habits

Let me share what a typical morning looked like during my "fake it till you make it" days. I'd wake up, immediately avoid checking my bank account (hello, scarcity mindset), scroll through social media comparing myself to everyone else's highlight reels, then try to Band-Aid my anxiety with some rushed affirmations.

Know what that got me? A prosperity consciousness that was about as stable as a house of cards in a hurricane. It wasn't until my cancer journey forced me to completely restructure my daily practices that I discovered what really creates lasting abundance awareness.

Today, my prosperity practice looks radically different. It started during those long hospital mornings when all I had was time and the choice of where to focus my consciousness. Instead of checking my phone first thing (partly because I was too weak to reach it), I started what I now call my "First Fifteen" - fifteen minutes of pure prosperity consciousness before the world gets a vote.

Let me walk you through what this actually looks like, not the Instagram version but the real, messy, human version. I grab my coffee (because let's be real, even prosperity teachers need their caffeine), and I sit in what I call my "abundance chair" - it's just an old armchair, but it's become my sacred space for consciousness work.

First, I do what I call my "Prosperity Scan." Instead of immediately looking for what's wrong or what needs fixing, I consciously notice what's working. The coffee in my cup? Abundance. The air in my lungs? Abundance. The early morning quiet? Pure abundance. This isn't just gratitude - it's actively training your consciousness to seek evidence of prosperity.

Here's where most people get tripped up - they think prosperity habits have to be perfect to be effective. During my early recovery days, I thought if I missed a morning meditation, the whole day was shot. Now I know better. Some mornings, my prosperity practice happens in the shower. Some days, it's while I'm stuck in traffic. The key isn't perfection - it's persistence.

I developed what I call the "Abundance Anchor" practice. Throughout the day, I have specific triggers that remind me to check my prosperity consciousness. Every time I reach for my wallet, I remind myself "There's always more where this came from." Every time I check my email, I pause first and affirm "I am open to receiving unexpected good."

These aren't just affirmations - they're pattern interrupts for scarcity thinking. Remember how I used to manifest money for drugs? That same focused intention now gets redirected into manifesting prosperity consciousness throughout my day.

One morning during my "First Fifteen," I had this insight that changed everything. I realized I was treating prosperity consciousness like a destination instead of a daily practice. It's like I told my Wednesday circle: "You don't get in shape by thinking about the gym - you have to actually show up and do the work."

This led me to create what I now teach as the "Daily Abundance Practice." Not another complicated spiritual to-do list, but a rhythm that naturally reinforces your prosperity consciousness throughout the day. Let me share how you can make this your own.

Your Daily Abundance Practice

Remember that old armchair I mentioned? You don't need special equipment or a perfect spiritual environment to do this. All you need is the willingness to show up for your prosperity consciousness every day, even if it's just for a few minutes at first.

Start with what I call your "Morning Power Portal" - the first fifteen minutes after you wake up. This is when your consciousness is most receptive. Instead of reaching for your phone (I know, it's hard - I still catch myself sometimes), take three deep breaths and ask yourself: "What flavor of abundance am I choosing to experience today?"

Here's the exact practice I use and teach:

First Foundation (Morning):
- Pour your coffee or tea mindfully (this is part of the practice, not just preparation)
- Find your abundance spot (mine's that old armchair)
- Take three conscious breaths
- Ask yourself: "Where is abundance already showing up in my life right now?"
- Write down the first three things that come to mind without censoring

I call the next part "Conscious Creation" - it's the bridge between your morning intention and your daily activities. This isn't about sitting in meditation for hours (though if you can, go for it). It's about creating momentum that carries your prosperity consciousness through your day.

Here's how it looks in real life. After my three abundance acknowledgments, I spend about five minutes feeling into my day ahead. Not planning it - feeling it. What opportunities might show up? What challenges might need my prosperity consciousness? I learned this during my cancer treatments when each day was unpredictable. Instead of trying to control outcomes, I started preparing my consciousness for whatever might arise.

Mid-Day Momentum (this is crucial - most people skip it):
- Set a reminder on your phone for your prosperity pause
- When it goes off, stop whatever you're doing
- Take one conscious breath
- Ask yourself: "What evidence of abundance have I noticed today?"
- Write down at least one thing, no matter how small

Here's what's fascinating - my students who practice this mid-day check-in consistently report more synchronicities and opportunities showing up. It's like telling the universe, "Yes, I'm paying attention to the abundance you're sending!"

Evening Integration (this is where the magic happens):
- Before bed, review your day through the lens of prosperity
- Note any moments where you maintained abundance consciousness through challenges
- Celebrate any unexpected good that showed up
- Set your intention for tomorrow's prosperity expression

Let me share something personal about this evening practice. During my darkest days of IRS debt, I would force myself to find at least one expression of abundance each day, even if it was just "I'm still breathing." Those tiny acknowledgments built a foundation for bigger manifestations.

The real power of this practice shows up after about 21 days - that's when it starts becoming your natural operating system rather than something you have to remember to do. But here's what nobody tells you about creating new prosperity habits: you'll probably mess up. I still have days when I fall into old scarcity patterns, but now I catch myself faster. If you want to really take this up a notch trying this weekly:

Weekly Wisdom Gathering:
- Take 30 minutes at the end of each week
- Review your prosperity notes
- Notice patterns of abundance
- Plan next week's conscious creation

I remember one week when everything seemed to be going wrong. My Texas AC broke during a heatwave, a speaking engagement got canceled, and my favorite coffee shop closed (I know, first world problems). But when I reviewed my week's prosperity notes, I saw how each "setback" had led to something better - including finding a new coffee shop where I met someone who became a key business connection. As you progress through these natural rhythms you can begin to see patterns. Taking stock each month reminds you of your shift in consciousness.

Monthly Momentum (this is your game-changer):
- Schedule a deeper dive into your prosperity consciousness
- Review your Evidence Journal
- Update your prosperity goals
- Strengthen your support connections

Here's what I want you to remember about maintaining your abundance mindset: it's not about being perfect. It's about being persistent. Every time you catch yourself in scarcity thinking and choose to shift back to prosperity consciousness, you're building spiritual muscle.

You've got everything you need to start right now. Not when your bank account looks better, not when your circumstances change - right now. Because prosperity consciousness isn't something you achieve. It's something you practice until it becomes who you are.

Remember that hospital bed where we started this chapter? That version of me couldn't imagine the life I'm living now. But she could take one conscious breath, notice one expression of abundance, make one choice to trust. That's all you need to begin.

Your abundance journey is unique to you. But these practices? They're universal. They work whether you're facing health challenges, financial stress, or just wanting to expand your prosperity consciousness to new levels. The only question is: are you ready to make prosperity consciousness your daily practice?

Start with your next breath. Notice one expression of abundance right now. You've already begun.

Chapter 11
BECOMING THE INNER BILLIONAIRE

Back when I was cooking up ways to finance my next fix, if you'd told me I'd one day be writing the conclusion of a book about becoming your Inner Billionaire, I'd have laughed so hard I might have dropped my crack pipe. But here's the thing about transformation - it has a wicked sense of humor and impeccable timing.

You've journeyed with me through every twist and turn of this prosperity path. We've broken free from scarcity's prison, healed those money wounds that felt older than time itself, and learned to speak abundance so fluently we could probably teach it as a second language. You've discovered how to set prosperity goals that make your inner critic gasp and your soul sing. You've built a foundation stronger than my old dealer's alibi.

But this final chapter isn't just about wrapping things up with a pretty prosperity bow. It's about that moment when everything you've learned stops being theory and becomes your living truth. When your Inner Billionaire stops being a concept you're reaching for and becomes who you simply are.

Think of this as your graduation ceremony from the University of Unlimited Possibility - except instead of a cap and gown, you get to wear your authentic power, and instead of a diploma, you get to claim your birthright of abundance.

No student loans required (trust me, I've had enough experience with debt for all of us).

Let me share with you the exact moment my own Inner Billionaire finally came out of hiding...

My Final Transformation Story

Let me tell you about the day my Inner Billionaire finally came out of hiding. I was sitting in my car outside the IRS building, hands shaking like I'd had one too many espressos, staring at the final settlement papers. The irony wasn't lost on me - here I was, about to be free of the very debt I'd once sworn would follow me to my grave (or at least to some tropical island with no extradition treaty).

After years of believing I was stuck in an eternal financial time-out, after countless nights wondering if I'd ever stop checking under my bed for IRS agents, after transforming from crack addict to cancer survivor to consciousness teacher - there I was. Free. Not just from the debt, but from something far more binding: the beliefs that had created it.

But here's the plot twist - my real transformation didn't happen in that parking lot. It didn't happen when my cancer went into remission, or even when I started making millions again. It happened during what I lovingly call my "year of nothing."

Picture this: I'm living on food stamps, counting pennies like they're winning lottery tickets, in an apartment so small my ego had to wait outside. And that's when it hit me - I was happier with nothing than I'd ever been with everything. Not because poverty was some romantic spiritual adventure (trust me, it's not), but because I finally understood something that changed everything: my Inner Billionaire had been there all along, just waiting for me to stop looking for her in my bank account.

Your Inner Billionaire

I remember the exact moment. I was eating a dinner I'd bought with food stamps (not exactly the caviar dreams I'd once had), when this profound peace washed over me. And no, it wasn't food coma. It was this bone-deep knowing that I was whole, complete, and abundant - regardless of my bank balance, my zip code, or the fact that my car made interesting noises in five different languages.

This wasn't your typical "everything happens for a reason" spiritual bypass. This was more like getting cosmic smacked upside the head with the truth: I hadn't lost everything - I'd been stripped down to my essential self. The self that was already abundant, already whole, already enough. Turns out my Inner Billionaire had been there all along, probably rolling her eyes at my decades-long scavenger hunt for external validation.

What happened next was like watching the universe hit the "abundance accelerator." Within days, opportunities started appearing out of nowhere. A call from someone who'd attended one of my workshops years before, wanting me to speak at their event. A former client reaching out about consulting work. Small miracles began multiplying faster than my old drug dealer could make change.

But here's the real miracle - I didn't need any of it to feel abundant. For the first time in my life, I wasn't chasing prosperity consciousness; I was living from it. The money, the opportunities, the success that followed? They were just external reflections of an internal shift that had already happened.

That's what I mean by your final transformation story. It's not about the external changes (though those are nice bonuses). It's about the moment you recognize your Inner Billionaire isn't something to become - it's someone you've always been. Like Dorothy in the Wizard of Oz, you've had the power all along. You just needed to wake up from the dream of scarcity to remember it.

Your moment might look different from mine. It might not involve the IRS, food stamps, or questionable car noises. But I promise you this - when it happens, you'll know. Because suddenly, all the striving stops. The needing stops. The proving stops. And what remains is just you, in all your abundant glory, finally home.

Let me tell you about some of the ripples this transformation created. And no, I'm not talking about the kind of ripples I used to cause when I was doing cannonballs in hotel pools (though those were impressive). I'm talking about what happens when one person's Inner Billionaire wakes up and decides to throw a party.

The Ripple Effect of Abundance

You know what's wild about stepping into your prosperity consciousness? It's like having a superpower you can't keep to yourself. Trust me, I tried. But abundance has this annoying habit of spreading faster than gossip at a small-town church social.

Take Maria - a woman who showed up at one of my workshops during my "food stamps to freedom" tour. She sat in the back row, arms crossed, wearing the kind of skeptical expression I used to reserve for sobriety checkpoints. Later she told me she only came because her sister threatened to post her high school yearbook photos online if she didn't.

Maria was drowning in debt that made my old IRS tab look like pocket change. But what really got me was the day she heard her teenage daughter tell a friend, "College isn't for people like us." In that moment, Maria realized her scarcity mindset wasn't just affecting her - it was creating a generational hand-me-down she never intended to pass on.

Two years later, Maria hadn't just transformed her own financial reality (though she did that too). She'd started a financial literacy program for teenage girls in her community. Her daughter? Just got accepted to three universities. Talk about a plot twist.

Or consider James, this corporate hotshot who came to my seminar expecting another "think and grow rich" pep talk. Instead, he had what I like to call a "prosperity paradigm blindside." (It's like a regular epiphany but with better branding.) He realized his fear-based management style wasn't just making his team miserable - it was putting a prosperity ceiling on his entire department.

Within six months of embracing his Inner Billionaire, James had transformed his leadership approach from "The Devil Wears Prada" to something more like "Mr. Rogers Goes to Wall Street." His team's productivity doubled, but more importantly, people stopped hiding in the bathroom when they saw him coming.

The ripples kept spreading. I've had students report that after embracing their Inner Billionaire, their dogs became less anxious, their plants started thriving, and their mother-in-laws became marginally less critical. Okay, maybe I'm exaggerating about the mother-in-laws, but you get the point. When you shift your consciousness, you shift the entire field around you.

This isn't just some woo-woo theory (though I've got enough crystals now to open a New Age shop). Quantum physics shows us that consciousness affects reality. When you step into your prosperity consciousness, you literally change the energetic frequency of everything around you. It's like upgrading from dial-up to fiber optic, but instead of faster cat videos, you get accelerated abundance.

But here's what really cooked my noodle about this ripple effect - it's not just about individual transformations. When you're operating from true prosperity consciousness, something bigger happens.

Start seeing opportunities everywhere, like a spiritual bloodhound with a PhD in abundance tracking. It's not that the opportunities weren't there before - you just had your prosperity blinders on.

Begin solving problems from curiosity instead of fear. Remember my cancer journey? Instead of asking "Why me?" I started asking "What's possible?" That shift alone changed not just my healing but how I could help others heal their relationship with abundance.

Create bridges instead of walls. The same mind that used to calculate how many grams I could get for my last twenty bucks now helps others build pathways to their own prosperity. Talk about a career change.

Naturally inspire others without even trying. People start asking you what's different, like you've discovered some secret prosperity moisturizer. (Spoiler alert: it's just your Inner Billionaire's glow.)

Paying it Forward

Now, when people ask me how I maintain my prosperity consciousness, my answer usually makes them spill their organic fair-trade coffee. I don't maintain it - I give it away. It's like that old parable about the loaves and fishes, except instead of multiplying bread, we're multiplying billionaire consciousness.

Think about it - during my drug days, I was a master at sharing my connections (albeit not the kind you'd put on a resume). Now, I share something far more valuable: the lived experience of transformation. When someone tells me they'll never get out of debt, I can say, "Let me tell you about the time I thought the IRS and I were in a permanent long- term relationship..."

This isn't about becoming some guru on a mountain (though I did once teach a prosperity workshop on a ski slope - don't ask). It's about recognizing that your journey, with all its face-plants and victories, is exactly what someone else needs to hear. Your rock bottom might be someone else's stepping stone.

Every time you:

Share your abundance mindset with your kids
(even when they're rolling their eyes)
Mentor someone through their own transformation
Model prosperity consciousness in your daily interactions
(yes, even at the DMV)
Create your own abundance circles
(way better than those old addiction circles, trust me)
Live as walking, talking proof of what's possible

You're not just transforming your own life - you're creating what I call "abundance cascades." It's like a spiritual pyramid scheme, except instead of losing money, everyone gains consciousness.

Living Your Highest Prosperity Potential

Speaking of spiritual pyramid schemes, let me tell you what happened the first time I really stepped into my highest prosperity potential. I was giving a talk in San Diego, CA and for once, I wasn't focused on the paycheck or trying to prove I belonged there. I wasn't thinking about how far I'd come from my crack house days or worrying if anyone could tell I used to calculate profits faster than their accountants. I was simply being me - fully, completely, unapologetically prosperous me.

That's when I realized something that hit me harder than my first recovery meeting: Your highest potential isn't a destination - it's an ever- expanding expression of who you already are. Every time you think you've hit your ceiling, your Inner Billionaire just laughs and says, "Honey, that's not a ceiling - it's a dance floor."

Remember when I told you about my "year of nothing"? That wasn't my lowest point - it was actually my highest potential in disguise, wearing food stamps like a costume. Because that's when I learned that prosperity isn't about what you have - it's about who you're being while you have it (or don't).

Here's what living your highest prosperity potential really looks like:

It's waking up each morning and instead of asking "What can I get?" asking "What can I become?" It's like my old dealer's mindset, but instead of chasing the next high, you're pursuing the next level of consciousness. (Way better for your teeth, by the way.)

It's maintaining your prosperity consciousness even when life throws you curveballs. Cancer? Check. IRS debt? Been there. Mother-in-law moving in? Okay, I haven't faced that one, but you get the point. Your Inner Billionaire doesn't take sick days.

It's recognizing that every challenge is just your prosperity consciousness going to the gym. When I was diagnosed with cancer, I could have seen it as a prosperity setback. Instead, it became my master class in maintaining abundance consciousness while wearing a hospital gown (not my best fashion moment, but definitely my most transformative).

But here's the real juice - your highest potential isn't just about you. It's about becoming a living, breathing invitation for others to step into their own greatness. Remember Sarah's daughter who thought college wasn't for "people like us"? Sarah's transformation didn't just change her family's future - it rippled out to create a whole new generation of prosperous thinkers.

You didn't read this book by accident. Those "random" synchronicities that led you here? That was your Inner Billionaire orchestrating the whole thing. And now that you've awakened this consciousness, you can't go back to playing small. It would be like trying to stuff a genie back in the bottle - messy and ultimately pointless.

Your highest prosperity potential is calling. It's whispering through your dreams, shouting through your desires, and probably sending you emoji-filled text messages by now. Listen to it. Trust it. Most importantly, act on it.

Don't dim your light to make others comfortable. Don't shrink your vision to fit in someone else's box. Don't settle for billionaire consciousness when your billionaire nature is ready to emerge. The world needs your full radiance, your complete expression, your total embodiment of prosperity consciousness.

This is your moment. This is your time. This is your invitation to play the biggest game possible. Your Inner Billionaire isn't just an idea - it's who you've always been, who you are, and who you're becoming.

The world is waiting for your light. Not just your reflection, but your full-spectrum, high-beam, stadium-floodlight brilliance. Share it boldly. Live it fully. Express it joyfully.

Because here's the truth I finally learned in that hospital bed, that IRS parking lot, that Australian speaking engagement: You are the prosperity you've been seeking. You are the abundance you've been chasing. You are the billionaire consciousness waiting to emerge.

Now go light up the world. Your Inner Billionaire has the matches ready.

ABOUT THE AUTHOR

Debbie Dobbins' journey from addiction to abundance reads more like a movie script than a typical success story. A former crack cocaine addict who transformed into an internationally recognized prosperity consciousness teacher, Debbie's life demonstrates the profound truth that our darkest moments often contain the seeds of our greatest purpose.

As a successful mortgage banker in Southern California, Debbie helped countless families achieve their dreams of homeownership while secretly battling addiction and a crushing IRS debt. Her personal breakthrough came through an unexpected combination of financial crisis, cancer diagnosis, and spiritual awakening that stripped away everything except what truly mattered - her innate connection to abundance.

Today, Debbie divides her time between Texas and the Caribbean, teaching prosperity principles to audiences worldwide. Her unique approach combines practical financial wisdom with profound spiritual truth, delivered with a raw honesty and humor that can only come from someone who has lived both extremes of the human experience.

Known for her ability to make complex prosperity principles accessible and actionable, Debbie has helped thousands transform their relationship with abundance through her workshops, retreats, and private coaching. Her work particularly resonates with women seeking to write their next life chapter, having walked that path herself.

A gifted storyteller and transformational teacher, Debbie brings together her experiences in the mortgage industry, her journey through addiction and recovery, and her deep understanding of prosperity consciousness to create lasting change in her clients' lives. Her message is simple yet profound: true prosperity isn't something we achieve - it's something we uncover by remembering who we've always been.

When not teaching or writing, Debbie can be found enjoying simple morning rituals with her coffee, practicing gratitude on Caribbean beaches, and proving that our greatest challenges often become our greatest gifts when viewed through the lens of prosperity consciousness.

Thanks for reading! Please add a short review on Amazon and let me know what you thought!

Did this book awaken something in you? Your Inner Billionaire is just getting started!

I'd be deeply grateful if you'd take a moment to share your thoughts about this book in a review. Your words might be exactly what another soul needs to hear to begin their own prosperity journey.

Ready to take your prosperity consciousness to the next level?

Visit www.debbiesdobbins.com/innerbillionaire to receive:
- "The Daily Prosperity Practice Guide"
- A practical roadmap for implementing the tools from this book
- Access to guided prosperity meditations
- Invitation to our private "Inner Billionaire" community
- Monthly prosperity consciousness updates

Want to work with me directly?
- Join my 6-week "Prosperity After 50" program
- Attend our transformational retreats
- Book a private prosperity consciousness session

Remember: Your Inner Billionaire isn't just a concept - it's who you truly are. Let's continue this journey together.

With infinite prosperity,
Debbie Dobbins

P.S. Follow my journey of prosperity consciousness in action:
Instagram: @debbiedobbins
Facebook: Debbie Dobbins
LinkedIn: Debbie Dobbins

www.ingramcontent.com/pod-product-compliance
Lightning Source LLC
Chambersburg PA
CBHW050636160426
43194CB00010B/1689